# GETTING TO NEUTRAL

# GETTING
## TO
# NEUTRAL

### HOW TO
### CONQUER NEGATIVITY AND
### THRIVE IN A CHAOTIC WORLD

## TREVOR MOAWAD

### WITH ANDY STAPLES

HarperOne
*An Imprint of HarperCollinsPublishers*

HarperCollins books may be purchased for educational, business, or sales promotional use. For information, please email the Special Markets Department at SPsales@harpercollins.com.

FIRST EDITION

Library of Congress Cataloging-in-Publication Data

Names: Moawad, Trevor, author.
Title: Getting to neutral : how to conquer negativity and thrive in a chaotic world / Trevor Moawad.
Description: 1 Edition. | San Francisco : HarperOne, 2022.
Identifiers: LCCN 2021033017 | ISBN 9780063111905 (hardcover) | ISBN 9780063111929 (ebook)
Subjects: LCSH: Attitude (Psychology) | Adjustment (Psychology) | Life skills.
Classification: LCC BF327 .M625 2022 | DDC 152.4—dc23
LC record available at https://lccn.loc.gov/2021033017

ISBN 978-0-06-311190-5
ISBN 978-0-06-323938-8 (ANZ)

22  23  24  25  26   LSC   10  9  8  7  6  5  4  3  2  1

TO ANYONE CLIMBING A MOUNTAIN

# CONTENTS

# FOREWORD

## —— BY CIARA ——

Trevor Moawad was my game-day sounding board. His job was to help my husband, Russell, prepare mentally to play the most demanding position in football, and once the game rolled around, Trevor and I would always sync up. It was as if we were playing the game ourselves. We would create our little team huddle. Trevor was the person I leaned on to stay neutral. We'd talk. We'd text. Afterward, we'd debrief.

Trevor was family, and I can't believe he's gone.

When you are a big dreamer and you seek a role that comes with a lot of pressure, there are going to be a lot of challenges. There is going to be a lot of adversity. It's not going to be easy. You have to accept that up front. I accepted it the first time I stood in front of a microphone and sang. Russell accepted it when he became the quarterback of the Seattle Seahawks.

In our house, we always say, "Pressure is a privilege." Trevor, who started working with Russell in 2012, used that phrase all the time. It means that what you're doing matters. But it's still pressure and the reality is that sometimes your human instincts get in the way. When the challenges come, your instincts might take you to a negative space. You can't stay there. You have to find neutral.

I don't like matching chaos with chaos. I don't like matching fire with fire. That's only going to make everything explode. When there is chaos, you have to come with opposite energy. There comes a point where being neutral is the only option. You have to go to that place, because otherwise it's impossible to get clarity and calm things down. I love the idea of taking a moment to pause and then going to neutral.

We have to be able to get to neutral, because we're all going to face adversity. We're going to get challenged along the way. We're going to have naysayers along the way. We're going to have doubters along the way. I've heard "no" more than I've heard "yes" along the way. I'm so proud to be where I am in my life, and I'm grateful for those "nos." As soon as you tell me "no," that's when the conversation really starts.

But even if you tell me "no," even if you tell me I can't succeed, I'm going to stay neutral. One of the best lines that the legendary Trevor Moawad gave me is that there's never been a statue of a critic. I love that. It couldn't get any truer than that. As long as I am able to execute my vision and feel really good about my art and my process, that's all I need. That's all there needs to be. If you're worried about what someone else has to say, it sends you all over the place. And the reality is that there is always going to be someone. There could be ninety-nine great comments, and there will always be one bad comment. But through the years, I've learned how to find my way to that neutral place that Trevor talks about.

Trevor was one of the best—if not *the* best—motivational speakers I've met. He always knew the right thing to say. Who you have feeding you in times of need makes a difference. Who you have feeding you matters when you're trying to navigate life's incredible journey. And when Trevor gave that vitamin dose of information to Russ, it fed my soul too.

I'm praying that this book will be the gift that keeps giving. Trevor planted so many seeds while he was here, and I believe those seeds will continue to blossom. He may be gone, but he can still change lives.

Even as he fought cancer at the end, he still knew how to find neutral. In our last conversations, he would start off each call crying. Then he'd find a moment when he just shifted to neutral, and by the end he was encouraging me.

But that was Trevor. He poured into everyone. He gave his all for everyone else. I know that God said to him, "Well done. I am pleased." God put Trevor on this earth to do exactly what he did. And we know that heaven has gained an angel.

# PREFACE

——— **BY ANDY STAPLES** ———

The email popped in on a Friday night in April 2021. Like many of the thousands of emails I received from Trevor in the course of writing two books together, this one contained a link and nothing more. Trevor had unearthed one more thing I needed to see to understand him—to help capture his voice. So I clicked.

This link led to a YouTube clip of Trevor's father, Bob, speaking to a rapt audience. Bob Moawad was a coach turned motivational speaker who could hold a crowd in the palm of his hand. He spent most of the last third of his life teaching people that a positive outlook would make their lives better. The speech Trevor had emailed me likely took place in 2006, about a year before Bob died following a long fight with cancer. Bob explained to the crowd that most people don't really expect an answer when they ask how we're doing, but he would give them one anyway.

"I'm vertical," Bob said. "I'm on this side of the carpet. I'm eating solid food. Who could ask for anything more?"

Trevor struggled for years to reconcile the fact that while his father was his hero, Trevor had built a similar business contradicting some of his father's core beliefs. Working with elite athletes, Trevor had learned that top performers need more than "just be positive." So he had developed a curriculum based on neutral thinking. And though that made him very successful, at times it made him sad. Deep down, Trevor wanted to be just like his dad, and he felt he had deviated from Bob's path. But as I watched that video, I heard Trevor. As Bob kept talking, I realized that what he and Trevor taught wasn't as different as Trevor feared.

*I'm vertical.*

*I'm on this side of the carpet.*

*I'm eating solid food.*

Those are neutral statements. Trevor always taught the athletes he worked with to go to the truth. Those were the facts at that moment. Bob Moawad was teaching neutral thinking years before his son put a name to it.

At the time Trevor sent that email, he had reached essentially the same point as his father had when that video was recorded. Both were fighting a battle against cancer that was far more difficult than they let on to the outside world. Both had only a few months left to live. Bob died about a year later. He was sixty-six. Trevor died September 15, 2021. He was forty-eight.

Trevor never told anyone he was dying. Like his former boss Nick Saban, he didn't believe in looking at the scoreboard. He chose instead to give each moment a life of its own. But beyond anything he taught, he undersold how serious his condition was because he cared more about the rest of us than he cared about himself. He didn't want me to give a single thought to his condition if it might take away even a second of joy from a moment with my family. Trevor didn't want Russell Wilson worrying about him when he could be trying to solve the Rams' defense. Trevor didn't want his friend Lawrence Frank to fret when he was trying to build a championship team with the Los Angeles Clippers.

He told a few of us the details of his cancer because he had to, but he kept that information from nearly everyone else because he preferred that they remain blissfully unaware. He worked most of the 2019 season with the Georgia football team while undergoing chemotherapy and various invasive procedures and didn't tell anyone in the organization about any of it until after the season ended. Trevor always felt his job was to serve others. If his clients were concerned about him, they were wasting mental energy that they could have used to improve their own performances. Originally, he didn't want to discuss his cancer fight in this book because it meant so many people would know. He only changed his mind when he realized that he could help so many people by passing along the lessons he learned during the process.

We finished the manuscript for this book at the end of May 2021.
After Trevor and I went over the last words over the phone and
I emailed the finished product to the publisher, I turned to my
wife. "I hope we didn't just write Trevor's last words," I said.
My wife works in medicine. As soon as I told her what kind of
cancer Trevor had back in 2019, she had warned me that he was
embarking on a fight few people win.

Trevor knew that too. But he refused to let the long odds drain
the life from him. He worked right through chemo. He pushed
himself to recover from surgeries. He rolled into radiation
focused only on the next step in the process.

Yes, there were moments he was afraid. Yes, there were times
he broke down and cried. Yes, there were times he thought the
world might crush him. But the beauty of Trevor was that he
never let those moments linger. He never let them drag him
into the abyss. Like Bob, who celebrated being vertical, Trevor
would find a fact to grab on to and climb back to level ground.
Maybe it was the privilege of taking a walk the following
morning with the Pacific Ocean as a backdrop. Maybe it was
his excitement that his friend Mel Tucker was using neutral
thinking to transform Michigan State's football program.

Trevor wouldn't want you to cry for him. He would want you
to live your best life. That's why we didn't change any of the
words in the body of the book after his passing. Trevor had
finally determined exactly how he wanted to teach neutral
thinking. He had developed a philosophy that had helped his
clients, but that philosophy also had sustained Trevor through a

fight against a disease that probably would have taken him even sooner had he not been so mentally tough.

I know Trevor walked through the Pearly Gates and into a bear hug from his dad. All Trevor ever wanted to do was make Bob proud, and he absolutely did. But Trevor did so much more than that.

It turns out we did write Trevor's last words, but I know they are the legacy Trevor wanted to leave. He wanted everyone to learn to think neutrally. He wanted us to celebrate that we're vertical and on this side of the carpet. He wanted us to stop worrying about the final score and just try to dominate every precious second we get on this planet.

# PROLOGUE

I woke up at 4:30 a.m. on September 7, 2019. A few hundred yards from my window, the Pacific Ocean lapped against the sand on Manhattan Beach. I was flying to Seattle to meet my client Russell Wilson the day before he opened his eighth NFL season.

The Seahawks were playing the Bengals at CenturyLink Field the next day. The plan for this particular Saturday was to meet with Russell and go through our usual pregame routine. I had made a video that would hammer home the importance of thinking neutrally. Neutral thinking replaces hardwired negativity, the kind of defeatist mindset that's nearly everybody's default. It's my own special innovation—a nonjudgmental, nonreactive way of coolly assessing problems and analyzing crises, a mode of attack that offers luminous clarity and supreme calm in the critical moments before taking decisive action. The beauty of Russell is that even though he understands the power of neutral thinking better than anyone, he also understands he needs to maintain his mental conditioning just as well as he does his physical conditioning. This pregame session would do for his brain what squats did for his thighs earlier in the week.

Meanwhile, I finally had the opportunity to slip back into my fall routine. I'd been in Nashville nine days earlier to watch the Georgia Bulldogs—one of my key college football clients since 2016—open their season with a win at Vanderbilt. Russell and the Seahawks had Super Bowl aspirations again. Coach Kirby Smart and his Bulldogs looked like contenders for the College Football Playoff. This could be a successful fall for everyone, which meant it could be a fun, rewarding fall for me. That's why I had gone to bed so excited the previous night. After a few years spent dealing with a divorce, I was finally about to have a football season where I could focus solely on the work. The roadblocks had all been removed.

So I rose before the sun that morning and started packing my bag. As I passed by the mirror, my brain registered something that wasn't quite right.

Why were my eyes yellow?

I turned on the light in the bathroom.

Why were my eyes REALLY fucking yellow?

My mind started spinning. What would cause this? I'd gotten dehydrated a few days earlier and drank a smoothie with turmeric in it. Could that be it? Turmeric is yellow. I'd had a stomach flare-up a few days before. Maybe it was a symptom of that. I did some googling, but nothing seemed obvious. I knew something was wrong, but I couldn't worry about it then. I needed to get to Seattle.

Corey Hart sang about wearing sunglasses at night. On that trip, I wore sunglasses whenever it was remotely socially acceptable. I wasn't hungover. I just didn't want anyone to see how yellow my eyes were. Other than that, I felt fine.

The following Thursday, I sat in a doctor's office back in California. Usually, I'm nervous in those settings. This time, I was relieved. I wanted to come up with a plan to find out why my body was acting so weird. Then I wanted to fix it. I wanted to ask the doctor if he could prescribe a pill to just get rid of the yellow in my eyes. "We need to figure out what's causing it," he said. "Usually, jaundice is a side effect of something else." Like preparing a team to make a Super Bowl run or to win an NBA title, we'd need to go through the process.

I'd been treated the previous February for a cut on the inside of my throat—an errant Cheez-It—and the doctor pulled up the past numbers. "Your enzymes were high, and your bilirubin was slightly elevated," he said. "Let's work off that." He had me schedule an ultrasound to see if I had a gallstone or a kidney stone. "And just to be safe," he added, "on Monday we'll get you an MRI."

I went in for the ultrasound. A nice older lady covered my stomach in that cold jelly and waved her wand across it.

She asked if I'd had jaundice before and she told me I'd be
fine. But I couldn't see what she was looking at. Was it a
tennis ball lodged in my abdomen? Was it nothing? I kept
reminding myself to deal with information as it was distributed
to me. This is a critical component of neutral thinking. In
that situation, it kept my imagination from running wild and
creating unnecessary anxiety. The next few weeks were a mix
of traveling for work—Philadelphia, New York, New Jersey,
Georgia, Florida—and visiting doctor's offices when I was back
in California. I got loaded into an MRI tube and lay there for
an hour. I had a Positron Emission Tomography (PET) scan,
which uses a dye containing radioactive tracers to examine how
your organs are functioning. Various doctors asked questions
and ordered tests and tried to collect as much information as
they could before giving me a verdict.

By that point, I hadn't had a full night's sleep in months. The
other physical oddity I noticed besides the jaundice was itching.
Night after night, I woke up with my legs begging to be
scratched. From just below my knees to the bottoms of my feet,
my skin screamed. Scratching my legs felt like a combination of
gratitude, victory, and sex. It felt like I'd won a gold medal. I'd
never been as relieved as in that moment between the scratch
and the itch flaring up again.

When the final verdict came back, I was summoned to another
doctor's office. He was still in surgery, so I spent almost two
hours in a room by myself waiting. There was a large exam
chair in the center of the room. It reclined and moved and
allowed the patient to be more comfortable during exams. It

had been freshly wrapped in paper just for me. That's where I was supposed to sit. I chose not to because that chair didn't make me more comfortable. The entire idea of it made me uncomfortable. I sat in one of the small chairs off to the side where visitors usually sat. By sitting there, I couldn't see what was on the doctor's computer screen. I couldn't see my chart. And I also didn't want to feel like I'd be there long. I wanted to feel like a temporary visitor, even though I already could tell I'd be spending more time in rooms like this one. Sitting there alone, I gave myself the kind of talk I give the athletes and coaches I work with. This is the intense one. Whatever it is, I'll get through it.

"It looks like we've got something going on in the gallbladder and the bile duct," the doctor said when he finally arrived.

He knew it was the C-word. What he didn't quite know yet was how to remove the offending cells. Did I have a tumor in my gallbladder? Did I have one in my bile duct? Did I have something in both places? I'd need to have a laparoscopic procedure (where they punch a hole in your skin to send a small camera into your body) to determine exactly what kind of surgery I'd need. It would take that procedure and three endoscopies (where they stick a camera on a tube down your esophagus like a plumber snaking out a clogged drain) to get the full picture of what I had.

By this point, I had a team of doctors working to rid me of the invader in my abdomen. My oncologist and my surgeon drew up a plan that would require chemotherapy throughout most of the fall to shrink my tumor, which was in my bile duct. Then, in February, I'd have a fairly invasive surgery to remove the rest. The prognosis for survival was good compared to a lot of cancers, but the treatment protocol would be a beast.

I had big plans for the fall of 2019. I'd moved from Arizona to one of the coolest places on Earth—the edge of the Pacific. We'd locked down the manuscript for my first book, and it was set to hit shelves in February of 2020. I had new clients and work that excited me. Who knew? Maybe I'd also meet someone. I hoped to build an entirely new life. Before I woke up that morning with yellow eyes, anything seemed possible.

By late October, I had a diagnosis and a treatment plan. As I stood listening to the waves crash onto Manhattan Beach one night, I mourned the end of the new life that had never really begun. "I just need to be calm," I told myself. "I just want to get better. I want to be able to sleep. I want this thing out of me."

I knew I'd need every lesson I'd taught the athletes and coaches I'd worked with through the years. I developed the concept of neutral thinking to help those people prepare and then perform their best under pressure, whether it was playing in the World Cup or playing in the Super Bowl with more than 100 million people watching. I distilled those lessons into a book to help those of us who aren't elite athletes take control of our lives by thinking neutrally. Now I needed to be more neutral than ever to face the toughest challenge of my life.

Little did I know that as I used neutral thinking to fight the C-word, another disease would emerge that would change the way we live and challenge us in ways we never imagined. To make it through a pandemic, we all needed to live neutrally.

If that combination of two horrific diseases taught me anything, it's that the world will keep throwing challenges at us. It doesn't care about our feelings. It also doesn't care if we're prepared. That's why we all need the tools to handle what comes next. This book will give you those tools.

In *It Takes What It Takes*, I introduced readers to concepts such as neutral thinking, the illusion of choice, and the negativity diet. I developed those concepts working with some of the best athletes in the world. These are people with incredible God-given talent who are always looking to gain an edge and be the best version of themselves when competition begins. With that book, I wanted to help people maximize their performance. Together, we turned good into better.

My first book outlined the concepts. This book gives you a practical, step-by-step guide to dealing with the various calamities the world will inevitably send your way. I'm serious about the practical part. I've been using these techniques to deal with the most serious personal crisis I've ever faced, so I can assure you they work. I'll start with lessons on how to handle stressful, life-altering situations. You'll learn to downshift your brain to neutral so you aren't trying to make critical decisions while your mind is redlining. Then

I'll explain how to choose the next right step when you've reached a neutral state.

After that, I'll show you how to take the steps to create a way of life that will allow you to find neutral quickly and be confident that you've chosen the correct next step. You'll examine your values. You'll examine your habits. You'll learn how to prepare for life events the way athletes prepare for a huge game.

Don't think of this book as a collection of pages. Think of it as a stack of lottery tickets. Living neutrally gives us a better chance to become who we are capable of—to win the battle of potential versus effectiveness. Instead of absorbing what the world dishes out, you'll know how to take the fight to adversity. To stand strong on substance. To be prepared to sustain the great even as you step into the scary.

# CHAPTER 1

# WHY NEUTRAL?

We locked in the words for *It Takes What It Takes* during the summer of 2019. Writing it had been a form of therapy for me. During much of the process, I was traveling across the country to work with various teams and businesses. Back at home in Phoenix, I was in the midst of a divorce. Drilling down on the principles of what I teach helped me live those principles during a period of extreme stress. Or at least it felt like extreme stress at the time. Late in 2019, after I had submitted the manuscript but before the book hit stores, I woke up with yellow eyes, a harbinger of some brutal months to come as I moved into 2020. The year 2020 would teach me I hadn't really known stress before.

As I recovered from major surgery and prepared for radiation treatment, a pandemic shut down the world. A new disease had crossed oceans. It was highly contagious. It was lethal in ways scientists initially struggled to understand. As doctors worked to learn as much as they could in an attempt to slow the spread of COVID-19, fear gripped those of us without medical degrees. We worried we might lose loved ones. We feared for our own health. And it wasn't only fear of the virus. We feared what might happen to our jobs as businesses were forced to pause and, in some cases, close. We feared what might happen to children as schools were forced to close. Some struggled with isolation. Many struggled financially. The negativity that I implored readers in the first book to avoid was inescapable. It enveloped the entire planet.

As we all struggled to get our footing in this new reality, I realized that dealing with the C-word (not COVID-19) *and* COVID-19 would require an even greater commitment to neutral thinking. Unlike when I taught the concepts to coaches and athletes, I wasn't trying to help a team go from decent to great. I was helping myself survive—to make it to the next day mentally intact. Meanwhile, I watched everyone else trying to manage through the pandemic and realized just how critical these skills are for all of us. Sure, they can help Russell Wilson try to reach the Super Bowl. But they also can help snap us out of a Groundhog Day loop. They can bring us back from the edge of a ruinous negative spiral.

Why not just be positive? When I speak to groups, a common question I get is "Why do you bash positive thinking?" I'm not bashing positive thinking by promoting neutral thinking. Sometimes positive thinking is just . . . impossible. And positive thinking with no basis for that positivity isn't helpful and, in some cases, can be hurtful. We can all agree that negative thinking only affects us negatively, but being less negative and being more positive are not synonymous. Positive thinking isn't the most effective antidote to negativity. Neutral thinking is.

*New York Times* writer David Leonhardt made this point implicitly in 2021 when discussing the pandemic. Some of the events of the first months of the pandemic hit people hardest who had initially believed that simply thinking positively would help the world deal with the disease in a more expedient fashion. (Note to everyone: viruses don't have feelings, nor do they care how *you* feel.) In March 2021, as people were being vaccinated and the idea of a "normal" existence began to feel real for the first time in a year, Leonhardt noted an uptick in skepticism toward the vaccine combined with a general feeling of hopelessness that sprang from a year of living with the virus. "The early coronavirus mistakes were mostly mistakes of excessive optimism," Leonhardt tweeted to his 147,000 followers.[1] "But that's not the only possible kind of public-health mistake. And at our current stage in the pandemic, undue pessimism has become as much of a problem as undue optimism."

The pandemic offers a hard lesson in why we have to remain neutral. I'm going to drill into your head that negative thinking needs to be avoided at all costs. If that's the only thing you take away from this book, you're profiting. But that isn't difficult to explain. Even without empirical data—of which there is plenty—you already know that thinking negatively can harm you. It's a little more difficult to explain why unearned positive thinking can be harmful at times. Norman Vincent Peale's 1952 book *The Power of Positive Thinking* has sold millions of copies and spawned a cottage industry of books, audio programs, business seminars, and tchotchkes that your most earnest friend probably kept on their desk at work (back when people had desks at an office). Positive thinking, in most cases, is a better alternative than negative thinking. But think back to the early days of the pandemic. Remember the magical thinking from politicians and pundits that the disease would simply disappear? Remember the theory—not supported by any research at the time—that the heat of summer would burn off the virus? The people who chose to believe that because they believed positivity would help eliminate the virus wound up being crushed the most when it became clear that none of that stuff was true. Those people wound up more negative and more depressed because positive thinking failed them.

Those people would have been much better off thinking neutrally. What, exactly, is neutral thinking? It's a method of making decisions that requires us to strip away our biases and focus on facts. It allows us to make decisions in a judgment-free manner that accepts what has happened in the past with an understanding that what happened before doesn't guarantee what will happen next. My friend Lawrence Frank is the president of basketball operations for the NBA's Los Angeles Clippers, and he explains this concept really well. "Just because you missed ten shots in a row doesn't mean the eleventh is going to be a miss," he says. "And just because you're ten-for-ten doesn't mean the next shot is going to be a make."

If we accept that the future isn't predetermined by the events of the past, we can dig deeper and understand that we can influence what happens next with our behaviors. We can accept that maybe we missed those ten shots in a row because we let our elbow flare out or because we didn't set our feet before rising to shoot. Recognizing and correcting those issues can help the next shot—and the one after that one—go through the net. Neutral thinking forces us to seek the truth. But it doesn't require us to render an opinion. If we missed ten shots in a row, it doesn't mean we stink at shooting a basketball. If we made ten shots in a row, it doesn't necessarily mean we are great at shooting a basketball. It means we need to comb through our personal shooting data to understand why we might have missed or made those shots. Did we alter our shooting stroke slightly? Are we allowing other concerns to distract us while we shoot? This information matters so much more than "I suck" or "I'm on fire." Those are judgments, and they have no place in neutral thinking. Other motivational systems encourage illusion or self-delusion. I never will.

I will show you how to accept what you've done in the past and understand that you control what happens in the future. Neutral thinking asks you to focus on the next set of steps in order to move forward. I'll teach you how to process information— good, bad, and otherwise—to help guide your behaviors. By opening this book, you've accepted a challenge. This isn't for everyone. There are a lot more people who want to believe everything will be okay instead of constantly analyzing their own personal data to ensure they are behaving in ways that will give them the tools to handle anything life throws their way.

But the people who believe in magical positive thinking will crumble when the doctor tells them they'll need yet another surgery and another round of radiation. They'll despair when the virus doesn't burn up in the heat of the summer. Meanwhile, the people who already think negatively will fall further down the hole in those moments. Those who stay neutral can persevere and even thrive.

It took me a while to come to neutral thinking—or at least to put a name to the practice I observed while working with championship athletes in football, soccer, baseball, basketball, and tennis. My father, Bob Moawad, was a nationally renowned motivational speaker. He produced programs that were taught in schools throughout the country and he leaned heavily into positive thinking. For a time, he was the president of the National Association for Self-Esteem. As a kid, I was my dad's personal lab rat. Every night I was warned of the dangers of "Stinkin' Thinkin'" and was required to repeat mantras and affirmations that essentially were attempts to speak achievements into existence.

So much of what my father taught relative to choosing a positive or negative approach never hit home with me, but as a young man, I tried to follow his teaching. As a team captain in high school soccer and basketball, I tried ceaselessly to convince my peers to be more positive and failed. As a soccer and basketball player at Occidental College, I was made fun of relentlessly for trying to get my peers "to believe" and be positive. As a high school teacher in Los Angeles and in Florida, I used my dad's "Unlocking Your Potential" curriculum.

I embedded positive psychology into my social sciences curriculum. But no matter how hard I tried, no matter how creative I got, I couldn't get more than about half the students to buy into those ideas. As a high school, club boys', and girls' soccer coach, I noticed some players gravitated to positivity. But if it wasn't in their wiring, they struggled to change and defaulted to negativity. As my career progressed, I watched national team members and global superstars struggle similarly. I understood why. I had felt exactly the way they did.

As I evolved from high school teacher/coach to sports psychology consultant to mental conditioning coach to director of performance at a school for the world's best athletes (IMG Academy in Bradenton, Florida) to college and pro sports consultant, the level of competitor kept rising and the percentage of the population willing to just "be positive" kept falling. I realized I couldn't sell the pivotal tenet that the personal development industry has pushed on all of us for years. And what is that? That your life, your world, your present, and your future will all get better if you embrace the power of positive thinking.

That simply is not true. The evidence doesn't support that. Your own personal experience doesn't support that. I joined tennis star Victoria Azarenka on her podcast in 2021,[2] and she sounded like many of the athletes I've worked with over the years. Vika, who has won the Australian Open twice and spent fifty-one weeks ranked No. 1 in the world, said the constant push to be positive always felt "cringey" to her. Her mind craved a different approach.

Most elite athletes never want to hear "Just be positive."
Whether they're training their bodies or their brains, they
want to know how, and they want specifics. Which lifts in
the weight room? How many reps of each? How many hours
of sleep per night? What temperature should the ice bath
be to reduce soreness tomorrow? How should I visualize
tomorrow's game? Should I play it all out in my mind or just
potential key moments?

Some of my clients tried to embrace positive thinking but
got frustrated and wound up stuck in the world's default
mentality—negative thinking. It's easier. It's safer. And we are
hardwired to assume the worst because we aren't that far along
in our evolution from a time (only a few thousand years ago)
when a negative consequence likely meant death. A 2001 study
by researchers from Case Western Reserve University and the
Free University of Amsterdam[3] examined multiple studies across
decades on such diverse topics as moods, sexual relations, and
the words teachers use when working with children. No matter
the topic, negative memories and negative experiences affected
people more deeply than their positive counterparts. "We
have found bad to be stronger than good in a disappointingly
relentless pattern," the study's authors concluded.

That's frustrating, but simply being positive wasn't a viable
alternative. Clients tuned out that messaging as well. I
understood my own educational platform remained largely
undeveloped against every athlete's toughest competitor:
negativity. It seeds self-doubt, fear, anxiety, cautiousness, and
hopelessness. If I'd said "Just be positive," those athletes would

have run for the doors like wannabe pre-med students run from organic chemistry.

As the years progressed, I stopped discussing positivity with the Jacksonville Jaguars or US soccer players or NFL draft trainees and focused on simpler tenets such as habit formation, behavior interpretation, goal direction, and conscious competency. There is a term for this: *anthropomaximology*. It started with the Soviet Union's Olympic machine in the 1970s. Basically, scientists studied what traits and habits made the best athletes and then prescribed those habits to developing athletes. If those traits—physical components such as speed and strength but also abstract concepts such as toughness or patience— could be nurtured in young athletes, then they would train even more efficiently and would have a massive advantage in competition. It turns out the Soviets also used tons of steroids. No one should copy that, but the mental piece of their training was worth examining and adapting. Anthropomaximology has evolved to mean the study of high achievers in any field, and it absolutely helps when trying to identify and build excellent habits. But I still needed a building block, a default mindset that would make my clients ready to accept the more advanced training that would come later.

I knew generally the direction I wanted to go, but I needed to codify it in a way I could explain and teach. That way, I could offer a specific set of guidelines that were much more palatable for that population to digest and apply. Around 2013, about when Vika was winning her second Aussie Open, I set the goal to find a way to teach a method of thinking that seemed to be the default mode of the best of the best in any field. I started out calling it "learning to be nonnegative," but I didn't teach any counter idea. The fact that being negative clearly and provably made you perform worse didn't mean that being positive worked the opposite way. From 2013 forward, I focused on helping clients understand the value of eliminating negativity.

Taylor Dent, or TD as his friends call him, is one of my all-time favorite athletes and people. He was a world-class tennis player who demanded a lawyerlike performance from his coaches. If you wanted him to do anything other than play tennis in order to help him get better at it, then you'd better be able to build a convincing case as to how your request would help him on the court. He was a prodigy—once identified as the next great American superstar—who in 2007 had to spend twenty-three hours a day in a body cast following back surgery. Then, when that surgery didn't work, he had another one. And then he came back to return to the top thirty in the world rankings. Taylor is a badass. Taylor's agent Oliver van Lindonk and I were friends, and Oliver brought me in behind the scenes to help sell TD on the new emerging forms of training that helped with injury prevention and overall fitness. These weren't really sport specific. If it connected to tennis, Taylor was on board. But if it was crazy leg kicks or bizarre stretches or running hills, Taylor would debate you on the merits of the training and send you running out of a room with your tail between your legs. He wanted to be convinced, and I loved it. Over time, Taylor and I became good friends. Over the years, I've leaned on a ton of world-class athletes or performers in order to stress-test different ideas. "Nonnegativity" made sense to him. It wasn't bullshit. He knew the less negative he could be on a court, the better he'd perform. If TD was convinced a concept worked, anyone could be convinced. That helped me realize I was moving in the right direction.

I added the idea of nonnegativity to our education manuals for Russell Wilson, the Memphis Grizzlies, Michigan football, Florida State football, and Alabama football. I added it into the sessions I taught at the army's Fort Bragg, at the Mayo Clinic and at EXOS, a training center frequented by pro athletes. I sat down and talked it through with coaches like Alabama's Nick Saban or Florida State's Jimbo Fisher or peers like Chad Bohling, who now serves as the mental conditioning coach for the New York Yankees and the Dallas Cowboys. I sought out articles and video clips to drive the point home and, among my clientele, the case for "less negative" became clearer.

As a teacher, what I recognized immediately were anecdotal wins like more head nodding, more attentive listening, longer attention spans, and less need for activities to keep everyone interested. The teaching platform could actually focus more on what the audience didn't do, didn't say, and didn't consume as opposed to a list of burdensome mainstays in peak performance world like positive affirmations, positive quotes, or the newly emerging mindfulness industry. It's an easy first step—or easier one—to NOT do something. Within Alabama football, which has won six national titles since Saban arrived, we identified a need to eliminate negative self-talk early in the process.

Through working with Nick and Jim McElwain at Colorado State, Jimbo Fisher at Florida State, Kirby Smart at Georgia, and Mel Tucker at Michigan State, I've refined that message into the kind of advice that will resonate with a nineteen-year-old football star: *Stop saying stupid shit out loud.* That may be blunt, but that population prefers bluntness. Players can understand that request and immediately begin applying it.

Why did this resonate? It's easy. There was no requirement to reach. There was largely no debate on the idea. People easily understood that their own negativity was a barrier to future success or a good reason to explain what's limited their past successes.

I understood that minimizing negativity was the most important thing I could teach to help athletes. I combined this training with an emphasis on great habits and behavior. I was continually teaching via case study, whether it was Olympic champion sprinter Usain Bolt or NFL quarterback Kurt Warner or rapper Drake, who decided at twenty-three that he would put $25 million in the bank by age twenty-five, made a plan, and accomplished that goal.

But no one ever says, "Let's be nonnegative." That would be a terrible rallying cry. I needed a way to combine the idea of flushing negativity with creating good behaviors, because those things truly are linked. When we remove negativity, it's like clearing the RAM on a computer. The machine (your brain) processes far more efficiently. But it's also important to use that newfound processing power to be more productive.

The mental architecture I had helped Nick Saban build at Alabama between 2007 and 2015 (including four national titles) showed that a great organization can combine and embrace these concepts. We had gotten players to stop staying negative things out loud, and then Nick had done an amazing job of creating an environment where players didn't think about championships or getting picked in the first round. He had convinced all these eighteen- to twenty-two-year-old stud athletes to focus exclusively on the task at hand. That could be a game, a workout, or a math test. Coaches never talked about winning the national championship. It was understood that such rewards would come if Crimson Tide players could win enough individual moments. If they allowed their gaze to drift too far into the future, they wouldn't be capable of dominating the next few seconds or minutes. Nick knew this, and he made sure he had a variety of different voices—including myself, motivational guru Kevin Elko, and Michigan State psychiatry professor Lonny Rosen, along with coaches and veteran players—sending the critical messages in different ways. One of Nick's superpowers is an understanding that not everyone hears the same message the same way. So he made sure he bombarded his players with the key messages—ditch the negativity, focus only on the next assignment—in as many different ways as he could. Every coach wants his team to take a season one game at a time. That's why that phrase is the most uttered cliché in the history of the profession. But most coaches can't get their players to actually do that. Nick not only gets them to take a season one game at a time; he convinces them to take their entire lives one moment at a time. Nick branded this mentality *The Process*. (He probably would get mad to hear it called branding, but Nick is *great* at branding.) If Tide players follow The Process, they don't get caught looking too far into the distance. They've followed it faithfully and, because of that, the program just keeps winning.

But in Nick's program, The Process is more of an all-consuming way of life. I definitely wanted clients to reach that point, but I wanted to start them off with something more digestible. I wanted to help them train their brains to adopt a similar mindset to the ones Alabama players adopted when they began to embrace The Process.

Russell Wilson provided a model for the mindset. We met in 2012 when he was training for the draft at IMG Academy. His agent Mark Rodgers usually handled professional baseball players. (Russell was an excellent baseball player who got drafted in 2010 by the Colorado Rockies in the fourth round.) Baseball was ahead of the curve in terms of mental conditioning, and Mark knew Russell could benefit from mental training. Russell was open to anything that could help him succeed in the NFL. We clicked immediately, and we've worked together ever since. As I watched Russell operate through the years, it was obvious he didn't allow his feelings to overtake his decision-making processes in moments of high stress or rousing success. Whether he threw four interceptions or four touchdowns, he still acted the same way the next time he set foot on the field. He assessed all the data from the previous plays in the game, but in that moment, as he relayed the next play to his teammates, he was in control of that play's outcome. As his mental conditioning coach, my job was to make sure he kept thinking that way. I also knew that if

I could help other clients learn to see the world this way, they could change their lives.

But again, "be nonnegative," while sound advice, is a lousy call to action. I needed a way to present that main idea and combine it with the traits I'd observed in Russell and other elite athletes. It needed to be easily understood by anyone. It also needed to emphasize the kind of inner peace that can come from shutting out negativity, avoiding unearned positivity, and getting to the truth.

I finally found it in 2015 while panting in my car at the base of a mountain at 7:30 on a June morning in Scottsdale, Arizona. My then-wife, Solange, and I were scrambling to get to Camelback Mountain for a hike. We loaded up with fluid backpacks, gels, and energy drinks, but we knew the thermometer wouldn't wait for us. As Arizona residents, we knew that in the summer, the window to exercise outside is between 5 a.m. and 8 a.m. when the heat is relatively manageable (which still might mean the high 80s). Wait until 8:30 a.m., and the heat feels like eight open ovens aimed at your entire body with every step you take. It's brutal. The Cholla side of Camelback is a worthy foe for accomplished hikers like Solange. It's a torture chamber for the more average ones like me. And when you go with Solange, getting to the top is mandatory.

Days earlier, I'd led fifteen New York Yankees staff members on the same trail. They were in town to play the Diamondbacks, and my friend and ex-partner Chad Bohling wanted to challenge his coworkers. We left their team hotel at 6:15 a.m.

The early hour made the heat much less of a competitor. Even then, I remember trying to keep up with Yankees manager Joe Girardi, a former Major League catcher-turned-CrossFitter. Even in the relative cool of the early morning, Joe wound up giving me the mercy look—the one that says, "I know you're trying."

"Trev, don't worry about being a great host and keeping up with me," he said. "I'll be good to go. Just take care of yourself and keep an eye on my other guys." Then he winked. All I could respond with was a thumbs-up. I couldn't sacrifice one breath to attempt to form words. The Cholla trail is as close as Arizona gets to Mount Kilimanjaro.

When I went with Solange, we didn't get to the trailhead until 8:15. The other locals were gone. Only tourists were dumb enough to be on the trail at this point. Solange popped out of our SUV and was gone. I eventually saw her at the top, but she had to wait thirty minutes for me to catch her. When I finally rolled my way onto a flat rock at the top, I realized I needed to relinquish the keys so she could get down—she literally bounded down—and start cooling off. I sat at the top stretching and regrouping. I had no idea in that moment how important this episode of poor time management would be to my own future in my profession.

The deep fatigue of the Arizona summer heat is rivaled only by noon football games in the Southeastern Conference (SEC). I tried to swallow, but there was no saliva to make anything move. The sweat pouring off me was the only way I knew I still had fluid in my body. I basically tumbled down the mountain. I stopped and slurped some water in the restroom. Then I slowly made my way down the hill to the car, where I finally got an accurate assessment of just how silly we'd been to hike that late in the morning.

The clock read 10:40. The thermometer? A whopping 111 degrees, on its way to hitting 118 later in the day. Solange popped open the trunk, and I stripped off my soaked shirt and hat and proceeded to alternately sip and dump four warm water bottles on myself.

"Damn," I said.

"Ridiculous," she said.

I got into the car and Solange pulled the heat shield away from the windshield. My head was down with the mass of my body leaning on the steering wheel. I was too tired to talk. All I could do was stare at the gear shift.

I started to shift into reverse to head home, but I realized I wasn't quite ready to drive yet, so I slid the gear to neutral. This particular model of Land Rover had a yellow light that highlighted the N on the column. As I stared at it, it struck me. NEUTRAL.

A vehicle in neutral is ready to move in any direction once the driver decides to put the car into gear. For humans, when energy is spent, when momentum is gone, shifting our brains to neutral allows us to regroup. As the air conditioner finally managed to blow some cool air on my face, it hit me. Neutral, in that moment, felt like a way to own the fact that we'd hiked way too late. We could get mad because we knew we should have gone earlier. We could assign blame because we felt like shit. Or we could accept that it happened, regroup, and position ourselves to move forward.

This was my flux capacitor moment. Getting into neutral had allowed me to go 88 miles an hour and join Doc Brown in the future. I finally had my call to action.

By 2017, I had incorporated the idea of neutral thinking into everything I taught. I had found something that took people away from negative but gave them something more useful than positive. Russell is neutral thinking's most fervent proselytizer, probably because he understands it so instinctively. In 2020, he led the Seahawks to a 35–30 win against the Patriots on Sunday Night Football. The game started terribly. Russell's second pass attempt got intercepted by Devin McCourty, who returned it for a touchdown. Eighty-one seconds in, Russell had put his team in a hole. But what matters is he didn't fall into that hole. He stayed neutral. So at the end of a game when he completed 75 percent of his passes and threw for five touchdowns (not counting McCourty's), Russell was asked in the postgame press conference how he managed to bounce back from the interception. His answer: he didn't need to bounce back because he never let himself bounce away in the first place.

"Obviously, that one play wasn't what we wanted, but there's a lot of game left and I go straight to neutral," Russell said. "I've always talked about being neutral—not being too high, not being too low. I understand that neutrality is going to allow me to be successful more times than not. I'm such a big believer in it. I think it's helped my career and my life, everything from the greatest moments to the toughest moments. Just being able to remain neutral allows me to just focus on the next play, the next moment."

When I teach neutral thinking outside the elite athlete population, sometimes I get initial pushback. That's understandable. We've had "be positive" drilled into our heads for a long time. When I tell you to think neutrally instead of positively, your natural response might be "But I don't want to be a robot." And I get it. We associate positivity and negativity with emotion. We associate neutral with simply being blank. Some have asked what the difference is between neutral thinking and nihilism. Nihilism is essentially a rejection of every belief system. It's a combination of pessimism and skepticism so extreme that its adopters tend to believe that life is meaningless. That is the exact opposite of what I want you to get from neutral thinking. I want you to use it to help create a vibrant, meaningful life.

Neutral thinking asks you to set emotion aside when you make decisions, but once you've made those decisions, I want you to live passionately. Love, celebrate, have faith. You can do all these things while still thinking neutrally. Shunning positive thinking doesn't mean you can't be optimistic. In fact, if you've used neutral thinking to adapt your behaviors to optimize your capabilities, you should be extremely optimistic about your future.

As I dealt with the C-word, neutral thinking gave me hope in times when I might have given in to despair. It allowed me to honestly appraise my situation. In the darkest moments, it provided the light. Everyone I've ever met would tell you that I couldn't be a robot if I tried, so I'm not going to recommend anything that takes away your passion.

Russell explained this concept in one sentence during a TED Talk in 2020.[4] "It's okay to have emotions," he said, "but don't be emotional." In other words, let the facts guide your decisions. Russell asks himself two questions: *What is the next step? How do I do this right here and right now?* When we've answered those questions, when we've made that decision and taken it to its outcome, we can cry or cheer or get mad or do a little dance. We're humans and these are perfectly natural reactions. But when the next decision needs to be made, shift back into neutral, evaluate the situation, and do it all over again.

In the world in which I teach, the operative question is: What can you do for us, this team, right now? For an individual athlete, it's: What can you do for yourself, right now? It's that simple for everyone else too. Can you make an honest catalogue of everything you've done to prepare yourself for this next moment and then use that information to guide your next decision? When you can, you're thinking neutrally.

If you read *It Takes What It Takes*, these next few pages will sound familiar, but I want to make sure our newcomers are grounded in the concepts I introduced in the first book. We'll explore many of these in more depth in the forthcoming chapters, but it's helpful to review the basic tenets.

## MAKE A PLAN

You don't have to be as audacious as Drake with his $25 million-in-the-bank plan, but it is important to have goals to work toward. The difference between thinking neutrally and being blindly positive is that you're going to ground your goals in facts, and you're going to create a set of achievable criteria along the way.

Anyone can say, "I'm going to run a marathon." But how many of us would actually finish those 26.2 miles? If you're relying on the power of positive thinking, you're telling yourself "I CAN DO IT." But can you? Have you ever run more than five miles at once, much less ten, fifteen, twenty, or twenty-five? If the answer to that last question is no, then the truth is you probably can't run 26.2 miles.

Right now.

And that's the key. A magical positive thinker might try a few long runs and then suddenly become a sullen negative thinker who says "I CAN'T DO IT" when the reality is that that person probably could run that distance if they took the required steps in the required order. A neutral thinker would say "The longest I've ever run at once is four miles. So what exactly do I need to do to build my stamina to make it possible to run 26.2?"

Then that neutral thinker would do some homework. They'd find out the best methods for building that stamina. They'd learn about varying distances throughout the week to maximize progression. They would study how much time it takes to properly train for a marathon and make sure they could. They'd learn about *fartlek*, which sounds like a wacky way to pass gas but really is a Swedish word that in the running community describes interval runs that mix faster pushes with slower recovery periods. On day one of training, they might run only three miles. They might not complete a ten-mile run for more than a month. But day by day, they'll be building a database upon which they can draw once race day comes.

When it finally is time to run those 26.2 miles, there will be nothing magical about the belief that finishing is possible. Nor will there be any negativity. Our neutral-thinking runner will stand at the start line thinking "When I did my twenty-mile training run a few weeks ago, I had gas left in the tank. I have my gel packs and protein bars with me. I'm going to stay hydrated." All that's left to do is run.

Your goal doesn't have to be as extreme as running a marathon. It can be to complete a nagging task at work. It can be to cook dinner for the kids four nights a week instead of buying fast food. If you make a plan and follow those steps, it will feel easier because your brain will remain in neutral.

## THE ILLUSION OF CHOICE

When I speak to groups, this is the concept people want to talk about most after the presentation. It resonates because it's the easiest to explain but the most difficult to pull off in real life.

When I introduce this concept, I ask my audience to imagine an apple in one hand and a bag of Doritos in the other. Those are my choices. But do I really have a choice in that scenario? Of course I'm supposed to eat the apple instead of the Doritos. But will I?

Let's be honest. We all pick the bag of Doritos sometimes. The key is to build our discipline to the point where we choose the apple most of the time.

We face these nonchoices every day. Do I go home and get some sleep or do I have one more beer? Do I go to the gym or keep watching TV? Do I finish this report for work or do I browse Amazon for a few minutes? If we're thinking neutrally, we're more aware of the consequences of the wrong choices. We know making the correct ones will help us in the long run, even if it means we're giving up instant gratification now.

## YOUR WORDS MATTER

The only thing worse than thinking negatively is speaking negatively. When you verbalize that negative thought, it multiplies its effect.

So just don't say "This sucks" or "It's too hot" or "We'll never get this finished." It will bring you down even further, and it'll bring down the people around you. Instead, opt for neutral language. "Here are the issues" is more productive than "This sucks." "It's 94 degrees, and I've accomplished tasks before when it was 94 degrees" produces a different mindset than "It's too hot." "Here's what we have left and here's how much time we have" allows for a lot more productive goal-setting than "We'll never finish" ever could.

So I'll say to you the same thing we taught all those football players: *Stop saying stupid shit out loud.*

## CONTROL YOUR INPUT

In *It Takes What It Takes*, I explained an experiment I did on myself a few years ago. I bombarded myself with negative inputs—sad country songs, heavy metal, cable news—to see how much it truly affected my mind.

It went poorly. I had intended to do this for a month. After twenty-six days, I was basically an emotional mud puddle. I had always recommended limiting negative noise, but after the experiment, I realized that its impact was even worse than I'd been telling my clients, so I began working with them on recognizing negative inputs and either changing or eliminating them. We'll discuss this much more later in this book.

The pandemic amplified negative noise to deafening levels, and we've got to make sure we don't let it drown out all our healthy, neutral thoughts.

## KNOW THYSELF

In *It Takes What It Takes*, I explained how NFL running back Fred Taylor reclaimed his career and made the most of some exceptional God-given gifts by taking a hard look at himself early in his pro career. In the early years of his NFL career, Fred had a reputation for being injury prone. He wanted to change that, so my then-partner Chad and I studied Fred's teammates who were playing on their second and third contracts—where the truly big money is—to learn how they reached that point. We noticed that all those players shared two things in common: they arrived at the facility at 6:30 a.m. and they ended each day in an ice bath after practice.

These sound like simple things, but they required a level of discipline that Fred hadn't embraced previously in his career. He had to do a thorough self-examination and figure out why he hadn't been doing those things. When he realized he was goofing off way too much and staying out way too late, he knew what he needed to do. He began arriving at 6:30 a.m. every day and he ended each day in an ice bath. Doing that required correcting the other behaviors, and suddenly everything changed. Fred wasn't getting sidetracked by nagging injuries anymore. He wound up playing thirteen seasons in the NFL and retired with 11,695 career rushing yards—good for No. 17 all-time.

To truly live neutrally, we have to be able to evaluate ourselves honestly. That isn't always the most pleasant experience, but it can lead to some important truths that allow us to form better habits and make better decisions going forward. That's how you become a badass like Vika Azarenka.

"When shit happens to you and you're like, 'Let's be positive. Let's be positive.' It's sometimes impossible to be positive. So

being neutral—not going into negativity—is very useful," Vika
said once after a match. "It's very simple. It's very hard to do,
because it's constant work. But it's very, very useful. I feel like I
start there and then I start to shift into a better energy."

Getting to neutral can sometimes be the hardest part. Next, I'll
show you how to shift to neutral when shit really hits the fan.

# CHAPTER 2

# HOW TO DOWNSHIFT TO NEUTRAL

This next section is about pain. It's about fear. It's about doubt. It's about mortality. It's about some scary fucking moments, times I wouldn't wish on anyone—ever. It is not about national titles or mentoring CEOs or military operators. This is about an opponent more intimidating than any Super Bowl favorite or world No. 1.

A few weeks after I woke up with yellow eyes in September 2019, I learned exactly why. I had cancer. Specifically, I had cholangio carcinoma, a cancer that starts in the bile duct. You won't see me write that word this way again after this paragraph. I prefer "the C-word" because the actual word carries so much negativity—and with good reason. The American Cancer Society estimated that about 1.9 million new cases would be diagnosed in America in 2021 and that about 1,670 Americans would die from cancer each day in 2021. It is a brutal, unflinching killer. It carries no prejudice. It doesn't care about timing. It doesn't care how much money you have. It doesn't care how many people follow you on Instagram. It is a heavyweight fighter that can be knocked out, but it will never, ever forfeit.

But you already know that. You may have watched it kill a loved one. You may have watched a loved one beat it. You may have fought it yourself. If you beat it, congratulations. I now know exactly how strong you had to be, and you're a badass. If you're fighting it now, keep fighting. I hope some of the techniques you'll read about in this book help you fight as much as they helped me fight.

Most of this book and its predecessor examine high-performance strategies through the lens of some of the most skilled, accomplished people in the world. We study how they navigate life neutrally, how they build plans and manage adversity and try to extract the clues that can help us in our own lives. This next part is about me—a guy fighting a disease that turned his world upside down. But the formulas I would need to execute aren't that different than the ones I'd teach a quarterback trying to reach the Super Bowl or an NBA point guard trying to lead his team to a title. It's the consequences that differ.

WAY too many of us have stared down the C-word and, as I learned through my experience, one battle can become multiple battles. I want you to understand this next concept through my eyes, through my journey. I'm not a Navy SEAL, nor am I a world-class athlete or multimillion-dollar CEO. But I am tough. I'm doing the best I can to make ends meet and keep taking steps forward.

I am grateful that everything I've ever taught equipped me to navigate the daily steps against this beast of an opponent. Everything I've ever learned was required. Everything. Following these steps wasn't a guarantee, but they gave me a chance to stay the course in a fight that had no shortcuts.

There's no fanfare. No cheering. It's you, your mind, and your body competing against something alien within you. What matters isn't everybody else's journey or outcomes or bullshit on the internet, but your own steps based upon how you execute the plan. The right mentality isn't reserved for athletes, military operators, and other high performers. It's universally available, but it's also required.

So how do you shift to neutral when it feels like everything is falling apart? It takes practice. Unfortunately for me, I got a lot more practice than I expected after that September 2019 morning when I woke up with yellow eyes. For me, the close of 2019 and the start of 2020 felt like a ceaseless cycle of doctor's appointments, medical procedures, and complications. Numerous tests led to a fairly logical conclusion, but that doesn't mean anyone is ever ready to hear they have the C-word. When I got my diagnosis on a Tuesday in September 2019, downshifting was the only way to manage the news.

The shift started with my choice of seats in the exam room.
Earlier, I explained why I wasn't sitting in the big chair usually
reserved for the patient. I didn't want to feel like I was taking
up permanent residence in that chair even though I would
spend plenty of time in chairs like it in the coming months.
To keep the proper mindset in that moment, this had to feel
like a temporary visit. Dr. Nicholas Nissen, who specializes in
surgeries involving the liver and the pancreas, sat down on a
rolling chair near the middle of the room. Around him were
three younger doctors shadowing his every move. From my seat
on the side, I couldn't see the computer screen. I couldn't see
my chart. This was also strategic. I wanted Dr. Nissen, who had
dealt with many cases like mine, to explain all the big words. I
didn't <u>want</u> to start googling terms that would probably only
scare me more. I wanted context from a person who understood
exactly what all those words meant.

I reminded myself to focus only on what I needed to do next.
Like our prospective marathon runner, I couldn't think about
the end of the course. This was especially true in this situation.
I figured the news would be bad. But I didn't know how
bad. At this point, moments before learning my diagnosis, I
couldn't worry about the finish line. I couldn't ponder the
latter stages of the race I was about to run. I could only focus
a few feet ahead of the start. I asked Dr. Nissen to help me
with that. I wanted only the information I absolutely needed
in that moment. Exploring too many possibilities could only
lead to more fear, more panic. I may have already written one
book about neutral thinking, but that doesn't make sitting in a
doctor's office expecting a C-word diagnosis any less terrifying.

These techniques help us manage these moments. They don't completely eliminate fear or doubt. They simply allow us to keep the proper frame of mind as we determine the next steps.

I listened as Dr. Nissen explained what was happening inside my body. "We're dealing with something in your gallbladder and something in your bile duct," he said. He didn't have to say "tumors." What I had was pretty rare, but I didn't need to know that at the time. It didn't matter. I really didn't even need to know the name. I didn't want to hear five-year survival rates or anything else that required me to look too far into the future. Psychologically, I needed to be in a place that was very low on information, low on long-term steps. I didn't ask what stage the C-word was in then, and I still haven't asked as I've dealt with the various steps of my treatment. You can google it if you want to learn all that stuff, but I wouldn't recommend it. For me, in that chair staring at those doctors, I needed a narrow focus to keep shifting into neutral. In a moment like that, every instinct we have tells us to look at the big picture; we have to work hard to zero in on the next move instead.

So I was very conscious of my next words. "Got it," I said. "I don't need to know anything other than your plan, Doc. What do you need from me to execute?"

Dr. Nissen told me they'd first need to perform a laparoscopic surgery that would help them map out my abdominal region. This involved punching holes in that area and using tubes outfitted with tiny cameras that would allow the doctors to explore and assess potential issues. After that, I'd start a course

of chemotherapy that would last for several months. If the
chemotherapy shrunk the tumors, then it would allow Dr.
Nissen to perform a more invasive surgery that would allow
him to remove all the problematic tissue. I asked how quickly
we could do the surgery, and Dr. Nissen said that would depend
on the effectiveness of the chemo drugs. Two months, he said,
wasn't unheard of. They would evaluate the efficacy of the
drugs following the first month, and then they would have a
better idea about when I'd have the surgery.

"I'm doing this mostly alone," I told Dr. Nissen. "What is the
best approach I can take?" Before he could answer, I told him
what my job was in sports. I said my mind could be an asset. I
told him my goal was to minimize negativity, and I gave a mini-
seminar on the power of less negative and on downshifting to
neutral. He thought that was fascinating.

"I need to live it now," I said.

He agreed, and then he said something that sounded like
some of the best coaches I've worked alongside. "Stay active,"
he said. "Trust the process." He chose this plan, he explained,
because his experience in similar cases made him believe it
would work. This sounded to me like a very neutral response.
Dr. Nissen went to the facts and to his experience and calmly
created a step-by-step plan for me. Surgeons aren't that
different from elite athletes. They must perform feats the
average person can't while under intense pressure—except their
successes and mistakes can have life-and-death consequences.
It makes sense that someone in that line of work would

gravitate toward a neutral, process-based mindset. Every step must be completed properly to obtain the desired outcome, so thinking too far past the next step is not usually useful. He knew I wanted to finish the treatment as soon as possible, but he wasn't going to skip any steps. When we knew the chemo had worked, then I could have the surgery. Hearing Dr. Nissen's natural inclination toward neutral thinking made me confident I had the right person quarterbacking my medical team. You can't walk into a doctor's office—particularly one where the doctor is one of the best in the country at what they do—and not get the truth. I didn't want positive bias or negative bias, and the team I had treating me wasn't going to give me that either. I appreciated that.

I wanted to get the laparoscopic procedure done as quickly as possible. Dr. Nissen said it could be scheduled in the next ten days. I repeated the advice he'd given me and added a piece of my own. "Stay active," I said. "Trust the process. Stay neutral."

I told him I still planned to work with my clients. That meant travel to Georgia and the rest of SEC country to join the Bulldogs. That meant going to Seattle to spend time with Russell. That meant going to Florida for spring training with the Mets. "There is no road map that works for every person," he said. "If you feel up to it, do it."

I walked out of Cedars-Sinai clearly aware of what was inside me. More important, I knew the next step. I needed to focus on how to stay strong through chemo. Healing and my health needed to move to No. 1 ahead of work on my priority list. I

called my assistant Jon and asked him to make four large signs
to keep in my condo. They needed to say BUILT FOR THIS. I
also had him put that motto on bag tags so I could see it when
I traveled.

Then I called my friend Lawrence Frank, who was an absolute
rock for me through the entire process. Lawrence has always
been a star in the basketball world even though he never even
made his high school team. As a high schooler in New Jersey,
Lawrence took notes on coaches he saw at elite recruiting
camps. He went to Indiana, where he served as a student
manager for notoriously fiery coach Bobby Knight. Knight
loved Lawrence so much that he recommended him to Kevin
O'Neill, who hired Lawrence as a twenty-two-year-old assistant
coach at Marquette in 1992 even though Lawrence hadn't
been a full-time coach before. Lawrence followed O'Neill
to Tennessee and then, in 1997, jumped to the NBA as an
assistant. In 2004, at age thirty-three, he was promoted to head
coach of the New Jersey Nets. Lawrence was a head coach in
New Jersey and Detroit and, between those stops, he served
as an assistant for coach Doc Rivers with the Celtics. Doc and
Lawrence reunited in 2014 with the Clippers and, in 2016,
Lawrence moved from the bench to the front office.

I met Lawrence through working with the Clippers and we
became fast friends. I had no idea how much he'd help me
in this process, though. Lawrence's wife, Susan, spent years
dealing with chronic illness, so Lawrence understood the
constant churn of appointments and treatments. He helped
me stay patient and he helped me stay neutral. When I called

Lawrence to give him the news Dr. Nissen had delivered to me, Lawrence confirmed that the plan was sound and reinforced that I had the right doctor in charge of my treatment. I'll go into a lot greater detail later about building the team that can help you stay neutral, but Lawrence was an all-star on my team.

After that, I drove to the Palos Verdes peninsula, a piece of land between Redondo Beach and Long Beach that juts west into the Pacific. It's covered in hills that allow for some spectacular ocean views. Many of those hills have stairs that allow hikers to climb more easily. I wanted to climb those stairs, to sweat out all the stress of the previous weeks, and stare out at the ocean. Dr. Nissen wanted me to stay active, and I would. The goal was to reach that bigger surgery, but I needed to focus on the steps that would get me to that surgery. But I had made my appointments. There was nothing else I could do in that moment. I had twenty-nine hours before I needed to be on a plane to join the Mets in Colorado, where they were playing the Rockies. All I could do was follow my doctor's advice and try to live the rest of that day with a high-functioning mentality.

LeBron James wore a hat a few years back in the NBA Finals that said THERE IS NO MAGIC PILL. That hat is 100 percent correct when it comes to basketball, and it definitely made sense as I stared down a long treatment plan. There is no one pill that just solves all our problems. Learning about the various medicines and procedures I'd need only drove home that point. I had downshifted to neutral to process the toughest appointment of my life. But learning the steps I'd need to take to treat the disease only reaffirmed that I'd need to *live* neutrally to make it through the coming months intact. Because there would be fear. There would be pain. These were unavoidable. But I had the tools to manage.

One of the challenges I faced early on was trying to hide my coloring while the doctors were attempting to figure out exactly what needed to be done. I didn't want anyone to see my yellow eyes, so I wore sunglasses whenever I could and tried never to go anywhere without a hat pulled low. I felt like I was living in shadow, but I didn't want my eyes to distract clients as I worked with them. When I joined the Mets in Denver after my diagnosis, I made sure I had my armor. One thing you learn dealing with Major League baseball players is that they're finely tuned athletes, but they can sometimes be highly judgmental. I wanted to keep the focus on the players and not on my situation.

Space was tough to find for meetings with players, so we'd find any place we could in storage closets or random side rooms. I brought my laptop and a plan, and we made some progress. After several of those closet meetings, the team headed out to the dugout to play the game, leaving me alone in the clubhouse. So I relaxed a little. I took off my hat and sunglasses, not realizing I was about to be seen without my protective gear.

First baseman Pete Alonso was nearing the end of a fantastic rookie season. Pete grew up in Tampa and starred at the University of Florida and, after a smooth two-year transition through the minor leagues, Pete came into the majors like he was shot out of a cannon. Pete was making a push for Rookie of the Year. On this day, he was tied with Ty Wigginton for the Mets' franchise record for hits by a rookie. At that point, he had hit forty-eight homers. That put him four behind the Yankees' Aaron Judge, who had set the Major League Baseball rookie record for homers two years earlier. With almost two weeks left in the season, Judge's record was in reach.

The Mets still had a chance to make the playoffs, so tension was high. I was watching on TV from the clubhouse in the sixth inning when Pete smoked a hanging curveball to the back of the left field stands in Coors Field for a solo home run to cut the Mets' deficit to 3–2 in a game they'd go on to win 7–4. That homer also broke the Mets' rookie hits record and tied Pete with Mark McGwire for No. 2 on the list of homers hit by a rookie. (Pete wound up breaking Judge's record by hitting fifty-three.) When Pete hit homer No. 49, I couldn't contain my enthusiasm. I ran down into the dugout—no hat, no sunglasses—to congratulate him when he crossed the plate. As I went up the stairs, I hit him with a huge high-five before heading back down the dugout stairs up to the clubhouse. Thirty seconds later I heard a voice . . .

"Trev!"

I had no idea who it was.

"Trev, come here!"

It was Pete. He looked at me and said, "Are you okay, bro?"

"Of course, Pete," I said.

"Your eyes don't look right, bud," Pete said. "Are you sure?"

I was stunned. This guy had just made history with a home run and he's asking me about my eyes.

"It's connected to some allergies and a few things that went south, but we are on our way to fixing it," I said. This wasn't exactly true, but I didn't want him worrying about me. "Thank you so much for caring, bro," I said. "Now get back to celebrating."

Pete did, but not before he said one more thing. "It's important for us," he said, "to take care of the people who take such good care of us."

I was stunned. It reminded me that I have an impact even when I don't immediately see it. It also made me realize how quickly I needed to go on offense against whatever I was facing.

Unfortunately for me, I didn't get to call all the plays on offense. After the procedure to map my abdomen, my doctors ordered me to take it easy. Chemotherapy wouldn't begin until November and I needed to heal from the first operation. I don't do "easy" well, and there were times that I let negativity and fear creep in. I had made fitness a critical piece of my daily routine and suddenly my runs had turned into slow walks because that's all I was allowed to do. I was forbidden to do pull-ups so my abdominal muscles could heal. Yoga was out for a while too.

In *It Takes What It Takes*, I explained that first you build your habits, then your habits build you. But sometimes factors completely out of our control destroy our routines. Our brains sometimes take that harder than our bodies. This was one of those times for me.

In some moments, I could yell "BUILT FOR THIS" and feel ready to conquer the world. In other moments, I broke down crying. Staying neutral requires vigilance, and I needed to keep reminding myself of that. I had a breakthrough in late October when I finally was allowed to take a yoga class again.

It was an ugly twenty-eight minutes. My downward dog was a shaggy mutt. My right-angle pose was probably more of an acute-angle pose. But I made it. And afterward, as endorphins surged through my body for the first time in what felt like forever, I realized that I needed to help my mind create that feeling even in moments when the endorphins weren't there to help. You have to create your own normalcy. It's possible to have a good day. It's possible to feel okay. I felt like Trevor Moawad, writer of a book, CEO of a company. I felt like that guy for the first time in a long time when I walked out of that yoga class. It was really empowering and uplifting for me to realize that I wasn't necessarily a victim. I was going to have good days. I needed that reminder, because it had been a long time since I'd had one.

I've never been one to catastrophize—to assume the absolute worst will happen. That goes against everything I teach, and it also goes against my nature. It's a terrible, inefficient, ineffective way to manage information. But sometimes information is so difficult to handle that we can't stop our brains from going to the darkest place. Sometimes, the information is so dramatic that we think our life is changed forever. So we overdramatize. We panic.

Depending on what we're dealing with, there may be clear truths that our lives will be in for some significant change. That certainly was the case for me. I had the C-word. I still needed chemotherapy, major surgery, and radiation. And that was the best-case scenario. So many things changed for me so fast. Those changes were physical, but I let them affect me mentally. The breakthrough came after that yoga class when I realized that EVERYTHING hadn't changed. I was still the same person. I still had friends. I still had a future. I could still find joy. Remember, neutral thinking isn't emotionless thinking. It's a way to process information to help make better decisions—decisions that lead to happiness, decisions that make you want to celebrate.

I wouldn't wish the stuff I went through from September 2019 to March 2020 on anyone. But starting that March, everyone else in the country would have to fight some of the same battles my mind had been fighting throughout my treatment. I'd dealt with fear, monotony, and loneliness for months, so, at that point, I was probably better prepared than most for what was about to happen. And I'm not sure most of us realized just how dramatically our lives would change until a game involving one of my former clients got canceled.

Chesapeake Energy Arena throbbed with the kind of energy only a giant crowd can bring. Oklahoma City Thunder dance team members were evenly distributed throughout the stands, clapping pom-poms above their heads as Zombie Nation's arena anthem "Kernkraft 400" surged through the building. You know it even if you don't know the name. Sing along with me. *OOOOOOOOO-OOOOOOOO, OOOOO-OOOOO, O, O-O, O-O, O-O.* Fans clapped and danced along as they waited for tipoff between the Thunder and the Utah Jazz. It was March 11, 2020, and those fans were about to be part of one of those "where were you" moments—except this moment had nothing to do with basketball.

I wasn't working with the Thunder anymore, but I remained close with their coach Billy Donovan. In this moment, Billy was still trying to help his team figure out how to stop Jazz star Donovan "Spider" Mitchell. Utah center Rudy Gobert was going to miss the game due to illness, so Thunder coaches and players conferenced on how that might change the Jazz offense from a schematic standpoint. The beat from that EDM classic still pulsated from the speakers hanging from the ceiling, but down on the court, something seemed amiss. Instead of gathering at midcourt for the tip-off, the teams remained huddled near their benches. The referees, meanwhile, huddled near the scorer's table.

In the wider world, news of a new, potentially deadly type of coronavirus had circulated for more than a month. Initial reports emerged from the Wuhan region of China in January. In February, an American-owned cruise ship called the *Diamond Princess* was quarantined in Japan after an outbreak on board. By early March, there were lockdowns in Europe and reports of cases in America, but we still had no real idea what that meant. The morning of the day the Jazz and Thunder were scheduled to play, actor Tom Hanks and his wife, Rita Wilson, revealed they had contracted the disease in Australia. Though other countries had told their citizens to stay in their homes to slow the spread of the virus, life in the United States still looked and felt close to normal.

That all changed that night in Oklahoma City. The referees called over Billy and Jazz coach Quin Snyder and told them to take their teams back to their locker rooms. Once everyone cleared the floor, Billy and Quin were called into a room beneath the arena where they met with an NBA official, who told the coaches that Gobert was out that night because he had tested positive for COVID-19.

"What's COVID-19?" the coaches asked.

At the time, *coronavirus* was the only word anyone outside the medical field used. Within weeks, we'd all know what COVID-19 and SARS-CoV-2 meant, but in early March 2020, everyone was learning on the fly. While this conversation happened in the bowels of the arena, the dance team had moved to the court and started throwing T-shirts to distract fans who had started to wonder just what the hell was going on. Shortly after, the public-address announcer took the mic.

*The game tonight has been postponed. You are all safe. Take your time in leaving the arena tonight and do so in an orderly fashion. Thank you for coming out tonight.*

By the end of the night, the NBA suspended its season. The following day, the NCAA canceled March Madness and various college leagues canceled the remainder of their conference tournaments. The rest of the country followed the lead of the sports world. By the end of that week, schools across America had shut down. Restaurants closed their dining rooms. Stores closed. So did gyms. By the end of the month, pretty much everyone except essential workers stayed home. Those who did leave probably were headed to a grocery store or pharmacy operating with a limited capacity. Looking back, that aborted game in Oklahoma City was the moment Americans began to realize life was about to change dramatically.

The pandemic mashed up a radically restricted lifestyle with a lack of in-person human interaction and fears about health and job security. It dropped an anxiety bomb on the entire planet. Negativity, which I teach all my clients to avoid as much as possible, suddenly was inescapable. It was a truly dangerous time, and not only because of a disease that would kill millions worldwide. The circumstances surrounding the pandemic made it easy to spiral into depression. Hopelessness mixed with fear and monotony created a toxic environment that needed to be managed. We needed to be able to downshift to neutral.

In the early days of the pandemic, a lot of well-meaning people suggested that simply staying positive would help. While that's usually harmless advice, in this particular case it was potentially disastrous. In late March and April 2020, we truly didn't know what was about to happen. Medical experts were still learning about the disease and couldn't offer any definitive answers, so no one knew how long this new way of living would last. This produced all manner of fear.

- Will I get COVID-19?

- Will I lose my job?

- Will I ever see my mom again?

These were real questions that millions of people found themselves asking day after interminable day. If you're trying to stay positive because the world says you must, you could say "Everything is going to be just fine soon." But what happened when it wasn't? Lots of people got COVID-19. Lots of people lost their jobs. Lots of people lost parents to the disease. Accepting false hope as a coping strategy only sets us up for a longer fall. The person who promised himself that everything would be just fine only dropped deeper into despair when he got his pay cut or when he got laid off because business dried up during the pandemic. The person who assumed, with no evidence, that everything would work out had to endure even more painful grief when she couldn't visit a dying parent in the hospital. Those situations are difficult enough with a perfect mindset; they're emotionally crippling when you've been tricking yourself into believing that some manner of magic will somehow take away all the bad things.

The early days of the pandemic felt similar to the period after my diagnosis. I knew life was going to change dramatically, but I wasn't sure exactly how or for how long. Such fears invite negativity, and it took me some time to understand that just because I couldn't live the way I lived before didn't mean I couldn't find happiness. Hopefully we'll never go through another pandemic in our lifetimes, but the memory of it is so fresh in all our minds that it can provide an excellent teaching tool.

We all remember how we felt in those first few days. It was bizarre. Streets were quiet. Skyscrapers that were once hives of activity sat mostly empty. Many of us watched the documentary about the weird people and the tigers on Netflix. At first, we hoped it would be over in a few weeks. We hoped we could "flatten the curve," as the medical experts said, and get back to normal life. But as those same experts learned more about the virus, it became clear we'd have to live in isolation for much, much longer.

You probably remember exactly how you felt when it dawned on you that normal life wasn't returning for a long time. As unpleasant as it may be, try to put yourself back in that time for a moment, because we're going to practice downshifting to neutral.

Fear reigned in those first few weeks. Your personal order may have differed slightly, but these were the major concerns for most people.

**A.  The virus itself.** We knew so little at the time about COVID-19. It was highly contagious but seemed to affect everyone differently. Some caught it and showed no symptoms at all. Some caught it and died within days. Doctors didn't yet know the best way to treat it, and there was a fear hospitals across the country would be overrun.

**B. Employment.** If we can't leave the house except to acquire essential supplies or get medical care, how will we get any work done? If we can't get any work done, how will our employers make money? If our employers can't make money, how will they pay us?

**C. Relatives and loved ones.** It did seem apparent even in those early days that COVID-19 was much deadlier for older populations than younger ones. So we worried about protecting those close to us who fell into this category.

**D. Children.** With schools closed, children stayed home. For those who still had to go to work—medical professionals or first responders, for example—who was going to take care of them? For everyone, how could those children continue learning if they didn't have school? How could parents work while trying to school their children?

Any one of these on its own would be considered a major adjustment. But all of these hit everyone at the same time. So fear was understandable. Negativity was everywhere. Still, neutral thinking remained possible. Here are the internal monologues that could (and did) help people downshift during a scary time. Much of this may sound like 20/20 hindsight now, but it's really more of a reminder to help you generate ideas if you find yourself in a similar situation in the future. The hope is we won't live through another pandemic, but there will be crises great and small. These ideas may help you navigate these times neutrally.

**A.** Going to the facts isn't easy when facts are scarce, which unfortunately was the case early in the pandemic. But we knew enough to start formulating a plan. Avoiding large groups was a must. Ditto for avoiding small, enclosed spaces with strangers. Keeping away from such situations could help alleviate fear of catching the disease. Yet we also knew that staying home with limited social interaction brought its own psychological peril, so to help downshift, we needed to find ways to stimulate our brains and bodies. We also needed to stay in contact with others. If you can get outside safely, do it. Get fresh air. Walk. Run. Move. If you're stuck inside, download a yoga app or an exercise program designed for hotel rooms (there are plenty). Meanwhile, set reminders to call—or even better, to FaceTime—friends and family members. They probably want to hear your voice as much as you want to hear theirs.

**B.** If you're an employee, get in touch with management and ask what you can do from home to help. If there is something you can do without being at the office, then keep doing it even if no one asks. This will show you're willing to pitch in during a time of crisis. It also will show off your ingenuity. It will also keep you from getting bored. If you're management, call your employees and check on them. Make sure they're okay. Let them know your main concern is their well-being. Extreme situations are usually temporary, but people remember how their bosses treated them during those situations. If you show you care, people will work harder for you. They'll also recommend you to other good potential employees.

**C.**  Call. Text. Skype. Zoom. Whatever you need to do to maintain interaction with these loved ones, do it. If they're afraid to go to the grocery store or the pharmacy and you live nearby, go for them. This will help alleviate their fear and give you something to do.

**D.**  For those parents who had to leave for work, finding childcare was critical. Family, friends, and neighbors helped one another a lot in this respect. Those parents working at home often found themselves serving as IT professionals when their kids couldn't connect to classes on Zoom. And even when they did get connected, it wasn't exactly a full school day. But there were other solutions that could help everyone in the house remain neutral. Encouraging creativity was one go-to solution. Handing out paper and markers and asking for a design to pin to the fridge can stimulate their brains. So can handing them an old smartphone and having them film and edit their own movie trailer. Kids are resilient, and they will usually try to find fun no matter the circumstances. They're good role models in that respect.

As you can see from these examples, the key is to focus on that next step and not the big picture. The pandemic proved the importance of this concept because, at first, we couldn't even conceive of how big the big picture actually was. Thinking about it could emotionally cripple us because of the overwhelming negativity. Positivity for the sake of positivity was even more dangerous, in some cases. We had to downshift or risk spiraling into the darkest of places.

I felt the same way when Dr. Nissen told me I had the C-word. That's why I asked him one key question: What do you need from me to execute?

The next time your world feels like it's collapsing around you, grab your mental gearshift and ask yourself something similar. Don't worry about the big picture. Ask this: What is the next thing I need to do?

You'll find yourself in neutral and ready to move in any direction.

# CHAPTER 3

# TAKING THE NEXT RIGHT STEP

When Si France was applying to medical school, someone asked him what he would do if he didn't get admitted. "I'm going to be a football coach," he said. France had just finished playing football at the University of Puget Sound in Tacoma, Washington. The person who asked the question thought the idea was ridiculous. France was dead serious. Then he got into medical school at Dartmouth, scuttling his coaching dreams.

After that, he went to Silicon Valley and worked as a consultant before starting his own company. That company, Welbe Health, offers an alternative to nursing homes that allows older people to have access to 24/7 care while still living in their own homes. Though he never did wind up coaching, Si is always on the lookout for lessons from the sports world that he can bring to his business. For him, the psychology of sports and the psychology of entrepreneurship are one and the same.

While on a cross-country skiing vacation in February 2020, Si heard me on several podcasts as I promoted *It Takes What It Takes*, so he picked up a copy. Only a few weeks after he read the book, he used it in a way I never imagined anyone would when I wrote it. I knew the concepts could translate to the business world, but Si used them to navigate a period when the difference between success and failure was literally life and death.

That March, Si was at one of his facilities near the San Jose airport when the news broke that several employees at the airport had tested positive for COVID-19. At the time, information about the disease was still spotty. But Si and Welbe Health's president Matt Patterson went on high alert. Their company served the most vulnerable population. "We care for very frail seniors," Si said. "We're just getting stats in from Wuhan. We don't know what to do." They had frontline workers on staff who needed to care for their clients while staying safe themselves. Si called his brother Del. Del was running operations for GCX Corporation, which manufactures equipment for hospital intensive care units and emergency rooms. Del told Si he'd been getting calls at all hours of the day and night from Asia and Europe asking for essentially ten years' worth of equipment overnight. What scared Si and Del most? Del hadn't gotten any such requests from within the United States yet. In other words, our country probably wasn't ready for what was coming. "We were in a panic," Si said, "and all of a sudden, we went neutral."

Matt, the Welbe Health president, used to be the medical director of the Naval Special Warfare Center. As the lead doctor for the Navy SEALs, Matt had already worked in plenty of high-pressure situations. He swung into action. Si began convening weekly all-hands meetings, and he decided the best way for the employees of Welbe Health to handle a constantly shifting landscape and a torrent of information and misinformation was to downshift to neutral and live there.

Neutral was the only acceptable option. Given the dire circumstances, there wasn't a way to be positive. But neutral can become a lifeline creating hope in a practical way. I've seen it as I've dealt with the C-word. There are few worse feelings than when the world hands you a set of circumstances that make positivity feel impossible. We all want to be there. No one asks to go negative. But sometimes it feels as if every force on the planet is pushing us there. Negative feels like the only place to land.

I get it. I've been there. But it isn't the only runway. There is another landing spot. Neutral can keep you from crashing. It can create a light in the darkness. The idea that you must be positive to have hope is bullshit. During my treatments, neutral thinking allowed me to build hope day by day—even on days when being positive wasn't even a remote possibility. Against the C-word, hope is a weapon. The same is true when a virus is rampaging across the world and your company has to stand between it and your customers.

In that first all-hands meeting, Si told his employees how to stay neutral. He told them to focus only on what they could control. He reminded them that they couldn't control every outcome. He told them to stop reading and watching the news if they wanted to avoid negativity. "Watch it for entertainment if you want," he said, "but the company has better information, and it will be shared with the employees." Si also told his employees not to rely on positivity either. This was going to be difficult and that was okay.

Si and his staff began giving the entire team a daily checklist.

- Read the plan of the day.

- Execute your assignment.

- Take care of your family.

Once everyone had downshifted, then it was time to figure out what to do next. For Si's company, that was a temporary change in business model. Welbe Health runs facilities that allow seniors to get a lot of the services they'd get at a nursing home, but then the clients return to their own homes instead of living in a managed-care facility. Si and his team realized that with a disease so contagious, they couldn't bring so many vulnerable people together in one place, so within a week, they converted to an entirely home-based model. Welbe Health put a tablet in each client's home that allowed clients and caregivers to access all the information they needed to provide the same level of care. They procured rapid COVID-19 tests so they could create mini-bubbles. Clients and caregivers took the tests before coming into contact with one another.

Si and his staff couldn't afford to look a year or two down the road. They kept repeating the same mantra: *We're going to do the best we can today*. They had to do that for their own sanity. "If you think about the stakes, it can be pretty overwhelming," Si said. "We're responsible for hundreds of employees and more than a thousand patients." In the early stages of the pandemic, the death rate among the population Si's company serves was close to 30 percent. Doctors were learning every day about how the disease worked and how it was treated, so thinking about the big picture was absolutely terrifying.

Si believes that staying neutral helped his company save lives. The statistics say that as of April 2021, sixty clients of Si's company should have died from COVID-19. Only ten had. "Fifty people are alive today," Si said. They're alive because Si and his dedicated staff took the next right step.

What's the next right step? It's the decision you make once you've downshifted to neutral and examined all the facts without judgment. The phrase itself comes from UCLA women's basketball coach Cori Close, who had to determine a lot of next right steps after the pandemic hit.

I met Cori when she worked as an assistant basketball coach at Florida State. I worked with the football team, but other coaches from across campus would drop in occasionally to share ideas. Cori was head coach Sue Semrau's top assistant, and it was obvious it wouldn't be long before she got a head-coaching job. So when she left Tallahassee in 2011 to become the head coach of UCLA's women's basketball team, it wasn't a surprise.

I was pleasantly surprised to hear from Cori in 2020, though. Her assistant Tasha Brown had read *It Takes What It Takes* and had recommended the book to Cori. *I know this guy*, Cori thought. So she reached out and asked if I'd have a Zoom session with her team, which was going through the off-season from hell.

Because of COVID-19 restrictions, the Bruins were one of the last teams in the country to get back to workouts. In a normal year, they'd work out throughout the summer and early fall to be ready for practice. UCLA couldn't work out until late September. Three players had opted out of the season. Meanwhile, freshmen Gemma Potter and Izzy Anstey, two top international recruits that Cori had hoped to plug into her lineup, were stuck at home in Australia because of immigration restrictions related to the pandemic. If you're counting, that's five players Cori expected to have on her roster who just went POOF. Basketball rosters aren't that big. That left the Bruins with eight players, and everyone around the UCLA program adopted the motto "Eight Is Enough," though Cori couldn't always have all eight at practice because of COVID-19 protocols.

Knowing it would be exceptionally difficult to do all the physical work required to be an elite team, Cori decided to increase her team's mental training. She asked her players to read *It Takes What It Takes* and after they did, she had them read it again and then split off into groups to present different ideas from the book to their teammates.

I'm honored Cori chose my book for her team because I know Cori has learned from the best. That's not hyperbole. Cori spent years learning from the person regarded by many coaches as the greatest coach in American sports history. When Cori was an assistant at UCLA in the 1990s, she established a relationship with former Bruins men's coach John Wooden. Wooden, who passed away in 2010, won ten national titles between 1964 and 1975. He won seven consecutive titles between 1967 and 1973, and his teams were a combined 205–5 during that stretch. But the reason most of the coaches in America have a John Wooden book on their shelves isn't because he won so much—it's because of the *way* he won.

Wooden was the ultimate neutral thinker. His signature visual aid was the Pyramid of Success, a fifteen-block triangle with five blocks underneath rows of four, three, two, and one blocks. The foundational principles in the blocks on the bottom are industriousness, friendship, loyalty, cooperation, and enthusiasm. The traits get more specific as you move further up the pyramid. Self-control is on the fourth row. Skill is on the third. Poise and confidence are on row two. The point of the pyramid is competitive greatness. Not winning—competitive greatness. John Wooden never wanted his players to think about the scoreboard. Wooden believed if his players mastered all the blocks on the pyramid, then the wins would take care of themselves. Wooden also figured that if the players mastered all those blocks, they'd wind up great employees, great bosses, great parents, and generally great people. What he taught remains beloved and respected because it is universal. Someone who masters initiative and alertness and then builds upon that by honing their skill and their team spirit can succeed in any environment.

Wooden's particular brand of process-oriented thinking influenced nearly all the coaches I've learned from in one form or another, but Cori got her lessons straight from the source. On Tuesdays when she was an assistant at UCLA and then at her alma mater UC-Santa Barbara, she met with Wooden and picked his brain. Wooden loved that Cori could get hot at times as a coach. He was always more stoic, but he tried to surround himself with people who produced more emotional energy. "He would say that's what his wife used to do all the time too," Cori said. "She'd bring all this passionate emotion, and they would bring it down to a simple next choice. And he would say that he needed that. He needed people around him who brought the fire."

Cori asked if she should tone that down as a coach. Wooden told her she shouldn't. "You are uniquely created to be the kind of coach you are," he told her. And that's an important point to remember. Whether you tend to be calm or fiery, quiet or loud, shy or extroverted, it doesn't matter. Just as coach Wooden's pyramid can work for everyone, neutral thinking can work for everyone. You already have everything you need. You only need to harness it and direct it.

Cori's team faced many situations during the 2020–2021 season that required a neutral approach. Positivity wouldn't help. Being positive isn't going to make the government change its mind and let your Australian players into the country. (Suing the government didn't work either. A group of international athletes at UCLA—including Potter and Anstey—tried that, and the case was dismissed.) Negativity could be downright dangerous, especially considering the sheer amount of obstacles thrown in the Bruins' way. There were times when the hurdles in the way of just playing a season seemed insurmountable to Cori, and those were the times she knew she needed to get back to neutral. Once Cori and her team learned how to downshift to neutral, they learned to lean on the truth to decide the next course of action.

"Neutral thinking, I think, is very parallel to what coach Wooden talked about," Cori said, "because coach Wooden never talked about the endgame. It was sort of inconsequential. It really had nothing to do with what we were doing in the moment."

Once you've learned to downshift, you can start putting those neutral thoughts to use. Just like coach Wooden, we're not looking at the scoreboard. We're trying to decide what we must do in the immediate moment. We accept what happened in the past, but we also accept that the future isn't predetermined. After learning to downshift to get yourself as far away as possible from the poles of negative and unearned positive thinking, this is the next most important skill you must learn if you want to live neutrally. You need to be able to determine your next right step.

Cori's team became excellent at that as that difficult season progressed. The Bruins collected and analyzed the data from their previous performances and discussed their successes and failures in neutral terms. The context of these conversations was learning how to downshift quickly when things didn't go their way during games and then make the correct choice for that next right step. On January 3, 2021, in Eugene, Oregon, Cori watched her players master these techniques in real time.

When the Bruins went to face 8–0 Oregon, they hadn't played in two weeks thanks to the cancellation of a game with Oregon State because of COVID protocols. So UCLA players and coaches had a long time to think about their 61–49 loss to Stanford on December 21, 2020. The Bruins had gotten within three points in the fourth quarter, but they never led at any point in the game and just couldn't get over the hump. Afterward, Cori and her players determined that Stanford— which would go on to win the national title that season—was the tougher, more together team in that game. But the Bruins could control all the things they didn't do well in that game. They didn't have an excuse for what happened. They got outrebounded 51–37. UCLA players could fight harder for rebounds. Stanford scored 34 points in the paint. The Bruins could front the post and not give up easy baskets when the ball got dumped inside.

In Eugene, UCLA would be the tougher, more together team because the Bruins would stay neutral. UCLA led by as many as 10 in the fourth quarter, but the Ducks kept punching back and cutting into the lead. Not long after Oregon rebounded a UCLA missed layup and raced down the floor for a Te-Hina Paopao layup to cut UCLA's lead to 2 with 2:25 remaining, the

Bruins assembled around their bench during a media timeout. This was a TV timeout, so Cori knew she had some time. So she let the players talk. Guard Lindsey Corsaro spoke up. "This is when neutral thinking counts," she said. "Right now. We practice this every day. Everybody ask themselves right now: 'What does this situation require of me?'"

The Bruins needed to get rebounds and they needed to switch the players they guarded if they got screened on the defensive end. All-America forward Michaela Onyenwere, the Bruins' best player, needed the ball in her hands if UCLA needed a big shot.

After two Oregon free throws tied the score, Onyenwere had her shot. She rose and fired from 3-point range.

She missed.

But Onyenwere followed her shot and grabbed the rebound (her 10th of the game). She then dropped in a layup (her 32nd and 33rd points) for the game winner. UCLA guard Charisma Osborne, who scored 22 points, explained to reporters after the game why Oregon's second-half scoring runs hadn't bothered the Bruins. "We didn't let that rattle us," she said. "We talk about staying neutral and moving on to the next play."

And on that next play, if you've chosen the next right step, you put yourself in a position to win. Cori said that after that game, there might have been a "NEU-TRAL THINK-ING" chant in the locker room. So take *that*, everyone who says you can't think neutrally and still be emotional.

That question Lindsey Corsaro asked of her teammates is the precise question we should all ask ourselves once we've downshifted to neutral. *What does this situation require of me?* It gets to the heart of the matter. It blocks out all the external distractions. It doesn't concern itself with what our teammates or our boss or our kid's teacher should be doing right now. Those things ultimately might affect whatever situation we're handling, but we can't control that. All we can control is what we do next.

What Lindsey asked her teammates is the purest form of the question I asked Dr. Nissen after he told me I had the C-word. *What do you need from me to execute?* I didn't ask what he was going to do. I didn't ask what the ultimate outcome might be. I wanted to know the next step in the plan and what I needed to do to keep the plan moving forward as scheduled.

If you lived through a serious health challenge or are living through one, you probably understand this better than the people around you who haven't. There is a broad desire from the outside to better process the how and why of what happened. I find those questions better suited for others. They are things a doctor can answer, but they aren't questions I asked very much. Truthfully, what really is in your control? I know what I can influence—my next step. Blood test. Meeting. Exercise. Scan. Treatment. Teleconference.

I can control my mentality. I can make sure I live neutrally. I can aggregate those things I can control and try to exert as much control over them as possible. I take this responsibility at the highest level. I'm the CEO of my company and of myself. This doesn't minimize any of the sense of urgency or intensity of what I'm facing. I know battling for one's life is not a football game or a Zoom meeting or a business venture. But managing the next move is universal. Execution may matter more depending on the event, but correctly identifying that next step is the best predictor of success. I can't tell you how gratifying it is when we get to that next step, and that gratification is hard earned.

Let's practice identifying that next step using a hypothetical situation. Imagine you've got a terrible coworker who bullies you every day and who is being exceptionally merciless today. This person just unleashed a torrent of insults on you, and you need to choose the next right step right now. These are the wrong questions to ask:

- Why is this person doing this to me?

There may be time to examine the issue more deeply later, but in the moment, the reason doesn't matter.

- How do I get out of here?

You have just as much right to be there as your bully. Don't let them chase you away.

- What can I say to make them feel as bad as they're making me feel?

Escalating the situation will only make it worse.

The correct question to ask—in this or any other stressful predicament—is Lindsey's question: *What does this situation require of me?*

This takes the bully out of your decision-making process as much as possible. You are worried about you, about *your* next step. You can't magically make this person better, but you can address the immediate situation. So you say this to the bully, "I don't appreciate being talked to like this, and it needs to stop now. If it continues, I'll be documenting it and presenting it to our supervisor and to human resources. This incident will be the first entry in my log."

With those three sentences, you have handled the situation as neutrally as possible. The person has been offered a choice. They can resolve the situation now or they can keep being a bully. If they choose the latter, you've already mapped out your next choice. So if the other person's behavior continues, you already know what the situation requires of you.

In 2020, I took part in an exceptional case study for choosing the next right step in a difficult, fluid situation. Mel Tucker, a coach I had worked with at Alabama, Georgia, and Colorado, had taken a new job as the head coach at Michigan State, and he asked me to help install the mental architecture for the program. Thanks to a confluence of circumstances that will probably never happen quite that way again, Mel got hired at the worst possible time a major college coach could get hired.

In February 2020, Mel had just finished his first season as the head coach at Colorado, and he was putting the finishing touches on his second recruiting class as the Buffaloes head coach. This was Mel's first head-coaching job after spending twenty-two years bouncing around the country as an assistant coach. He'd gone 5–7 that first year, but he was bringing in good players and seemed ready to turn the program around.

Meanwhile, in East Lansing, Michigan, Michigan State coach Mark Dantonio decided he couldn't promise recruits that he'd be the head coach for their entire careers. Dantonio realized this meant he needed to retire and let someone else lead the program. Typically, this sort of decision gets made in November and a school can choose from a fairly large pool of candidates finishing their seasons. The outgoing head coach works the bowl game and gets celebrated, and then there is a smooth handoff immediately after. In Michigan State's situation, Dantonio decided to step down on February 4, the day before National Signing Day, when high schoolers are allowed to sign their letters-of-intent for major college football programs. That meant Michigan State would have to try to hire a coach from a pool of people who had just wooed a new group of players to their current employer.

Needless to say, not many coaches who would be qualified to take over at a program like Michigan State wanted to make the move under those circumstances. Mel was one no different. When the Spartans approached him the first time, he turned them down to stay at Colorado. But a few days later, Michigan State officials came back. They offered to more than double

Mel's salary. And they offered a massive salary pool that would allow him to hire great assistants and pay them enough to keep them from leaving for similar jobs at other schools. They offered him the resources to essentially remake the program as he saw fit. Though Mel knew he'd get crushed for leaving Colorado after a year, it was too much to turn down. Plus, Mel is an Ohio native who played at Wisconsin. The Big Ten Conference is in his blood.

So he took the job. Unlike other first-year coaches, he wouldn't be able to choose his freshman class. Those players had already signed, expecting to play for Dantonio. He didn't yet have a strength-and-conditioning program in place during a crucial time for off-season workouts. He'd have to do all of that on the fly and then try to get to know the players on his roster during spring practice.

Then, about a month after Mel was hired and four days before spring practice was supposed to begin, the Big Ten shut down all sports activities because of the pandemic. Spring practice got wiped out. So did much of the off-season conditioning program. And that was only the start of the drama.

The players came back together for socially distanced workouts in June, and the Big Ten moved ahead with a plan to play a shortened, conference-game-only regular season. Then, in August, that plan changed. An Indiana player had been diagnosed with myocarditis—an inflammation of the heart muscle—after recovering from a bout with COVID-19. Though myocarditis is a potential side effect of any serious respiratory infection, Big Ten leaders worried about going ahead with a football season without hard data on the likelihood of developing the condition after a case of COVID-19. So, on August 11, 2020, the Big Ten pulled the plug. The season would be postponed indefinitely. Maybe it would start later. Maybe it would get played in the spring.

Several other leagues, including the Pac-12, the Mountain West, and the Mid-American Conferences, had made the same decision. But the Atlantic Coast (ACC), the Big 12, and the Southeastern Conferences (SEC) chose not to postpone. Their leaders said they would gather more data and postpone if necessary, but they planned to play their seasons if they could.

Mel had to manage a lot at this point. He still didn't know his players. They still didn't know him. And not everyone agreed on the next step. Some players wanted to play and were furious that the presidents of the schools in the conference would postpone the season. Other players feared staying on campus and continuing workouts because they didn't want to catch COVID-19 and potentially pass it along to vulnerable family members. Some players had parents or close relatives who had gotten very sick. Meanwhile, the medical information and the regulations changed every day. That's not an exaggeration. For months, Mel had to make sure he and his staff followed constantly shifting regulations handed down by the state of Michigan, by Ingham County, by Michigan State University, by the Big Ten, and by the NCAA. Mel repeatedly told his staff to stop trying to judge the ever-shifting regulations. It didn't matter if they were good, bad, or otherwise. Go to the facts. Can players come back to campus? No? Then let's find a way to help them stay in shape using stuff they have around the house since the gyms are probably closed where they live. After the players could return to campus, were they allowed to lift weights? Yes, but only in small, socially distanced groups? Okay. Then let's do that.

Mel had to juggle the concerns of the players and their families and the regulations while also trying to recruit new players to a school he hadn't had a chance to learn much about because of the shutdown. (And the NCAA kept adjusting the recruiting rules too.) Summer camps got wiped out, costing Mel and his staff a chance to meet and evaluate high schoolers that they might want to recruit at some point in the next few years. Everything a new coach needs to do, Mel couldn't do. But at least he didn't have to worry about preparing a team he didn't know for a season.

Until he did.

On September 16, 2020, after more than a month of protests from players, parents, and fans and after watching the ACC, the Big 12, and the NFL kick off their seasons, Big Ten presidents relented and reversed their decision. Teams would play an eight-game season starting on October 24.

Ready or not, Mel and the Spartans were going to play.

They worked their way through a weird, truncated preseason practice governed by a hodgepodge of regulations and hampered by the limited availability of players because of positive tests and contact tracing. When they finally took the field on October 24, the opponent was Rutgers, which typically is the Big Ten's resident doormat.

Mel's first game couldn't have started much worse. The Scarlet Knights drove for a touchdown. Then Michigan State fumbled and Rutgers recovered at the Spartans' 1-yard line and punched in a touchdown a few plays later. Not long after, Rutgers intercepted a Michigan State pass and returned it to the Michigan State 23-yard line. Two plays later, another touchdown. The 38–27 loss set off alarms in East Lansing. Michigan State is never supposed to lose to Rutgers. But the following week, those fears of disaster calmed when Michigan State quarterback Rocky Lombardi threw for 323 yards and the Spartans beat hated rival Michigan 27–24. For the moment, the pressure shifted to Ann Arbor, where veteran Michigan coach Jim Harbaugh was going through an equally tough stretch without the mitigating factor of being hired a few weeks before a pandemic hit.

But the external panic over Mel's team returned after a 49–7 loss at Iowa and a 24–0 loss to Indiana. Against Indiana, everything that possibly could have gone wrong went wrong early. In the first quarter, the Hoosiers intercepted a Michigan State pass and drove down the field for a touchdown. The Spartans fumbled on their next possession, and Indiana turned that turnover into a touchdown. With a defense as good as Indiana's and an offense as inconsistent as Michigan State's, a two-touchdown lead was plenty. Suddenly all the momentum from the Michigan win was gone.

What had happened? Had the Spartans just gotten lucky against the Wolverines? A game against Maryland the following Saturday felt like a more even matchup. But on that Thursday, Maryland announced that it couldn't play the game. Fifteen players had tested positive for COVID-19. So had seven staff members, including head coach Mike Locksley. Suddenly, Michigan State's next game would be against Northwestern. So much for an even matchup to get things back on track.

The Wildcats were 5–0, and they had just beaten Wisconsin to all but wrap up the Big Ten West title. They would be by far the best team Michigan State had played to that point.

Two days before Thanksgiving, Mel met the media to face questions about the game against Northwestern. He used some words you should be familiar with by now. "Our players and staff have done a formidable job just leaning into the new normal with what we've had to deal with every day in terms of trying to train, practice, play, and coach in this environment," he said. "We've managed to stay neutral. We understand what the facts are and what the truth is. Based upon that information, what do we need to do to give ourselves the best chance to practice and play as a football team?"

You'll notice that Mel said "to practice and play." Because just practicing had felt like moving heaven and earth at times. But Mel was trying everything he could to help the Spartans come together. He had missed critical culture-building time because of the timing of the coaching change. He had missed more because of the pandemic. Now he was about to send them out to play one of the nation's ultimate culture teams.

Northwestern doesn't sign the highest-rated recruits, but coach Pat Fitzgerald—a proud Northwestern alum—has worked at the school since 2001. He knows exactly what kind of players will fit in on the field and in the locker room. The Wildcats have spent most of this century building a program where the older players teach the younger ones the next right step, and that's why they routinely outplay expectations.

Mel wants to build that in East Lansing. The Wildcats have great habits, and Mel hopes the Spartans will also after they've played in his program for a while. "If you want to be good, there are certain things you have to do day in and day out," Mel said. "There are very few choices." He even used the phrase "the illusion of choice." When Mel has been in East Lansing a few years, his players will know those next right steps, and they'll make the correct decisions on those choices that aren't really choices.

But now Mel needed a spark to convince his team that all this talk of process and limited choices would eventually bear fruit, so he went to the film and he found the truth. The first half of the Indiana game was as awful an abomination as the score made it seem. But the second half was something different. The Spartans had played the Hoosiers to a 0–0 tie. Michigan State's defense had held Indiana's offense to 3.3 yards a play

in the second half. That wasn't just adequate. It was excellent.
Mel thought back to when he worked for Jim Tressel at Ohio
State in 2001. It was the staff's first year in Columbus, and
the Buckeyes had gotten beat 20–17 by Mel's alma mater
Wisconsin to fall to 3–2. The loss had been a collapse; Ohio
State had gone up 17–0 and Wisconsin had come back while
shutting out the Buckeyes the rest of the way. It was the kind of
loss that could destroy a season. But Tressel wouldn't let it. When
he entered the first staff meeting after the game, Tressel pointed
out that Ohio State had averaged more than 5 yards a carry the
last few times the Buckeyes' offense had run Tressel's favorite
play, which is called *Power*. Tressel wanted coaches to be honest
with their players about when they had made mistakes, but he
also wanted to make sure they pointed out what the players did
well. The message? This is not a total loss. There are aspects of
the game we do well, and we can build upon them. The Buckeyes
weren't perfect the rest of the way, but they ended that 2001
season by shocking favored Michigan in a preview of things to
come. In 2002, they went 14–0 and won the national title.

In 2020, Mel would hang the Spartans' next step on that
second-half defensive performance. The season didn't have to
be a total loss. Michigan State had deficiencies, but the Spartans
also could play in spurts in ways that would allow them to
compete with anyone. The trick was to turn those spurts into
longer stretches that produced wins.

Mel thought back to a section of *It Takes What It Takes* that
describes the levels of competence. You probably were taught
that those levels look like this.

- Unconscious incompetence: You don't know that you don't know how to succeed.

- Conscious incompetence: You know you don't know how to succeed.

- Conscious competence: You're succeeding, but you have to concentrate hard to perform your task correctly.

- Unconscious competence: You've completed the task so many times you can do it successfully without even thinking about it.

It can't work that way in the sports world because success requires so much conscious repetition. So the last two categories look like this in the world of living neutrally:

- Unconscious competence: You can succeed, but you aren't entirely sure why you're successful when you are.

- Conscious competence: You know the steps required for success, and you can repeat them.

As he rewatched the second half of the Indiana game, Mel saw an unconsciously competent team. But the beauty of unconscious competence in sports is that once you have some success—even if you don't know why you were successful—then you can pore over the video to determine exactly why you succeeded in certain situations. Mel saw a defensive line that could be tough to move at times. He saw linebackers that, when they remembered which gap to attack based on the play call, could make plays when those defensive linemen clogged up the point of attack.

Mel avoided negativity. The players knew they got shut out by Indiana. They didn't need to be dragged for that. He also avoided positivity. Believing they could beat Northwestern alone wouldn't make the Spartans capable of beating the Wildcats. They needed a plan. And the plan was to repeatedly reinforce what Michigan State did well with the hope that the players would take another step toward conscious competence.

The first major test came on Northwestern's first drive. The Wildcats moved the ball fairly easily down the field until they got just inside the Michigan State 20-yard line. After the Spartans held Northwestern to a 1-yard gain on third-and-2, Fitzgerald decided to go for it on fourth-and-1. He wanted to establish a tone. Instead, the Spartans established one. Michigan State's defensive tackles submarined the interior of Northwestern's offensive line, pushing all three players back toward the quarterback. Northwestern's Isaiah Bowser took the handoff, but he had no chance. Michigan State linebacker Antjuan Simmons came flying into a gap cleared by the defensive line and stuffed Bowser for no gain.

Two plays later, Lombardi hit Jalen Nailor down the left sideline for a 75-yard touchdown. Michigan State turned two interceptions into field goals and a fumble recovery into a touchdown, and the Spartans rolled to a 29–20 win.

Mel was right. The defense repeated its success from the second half of the Indiana game for an entire game, and the result was a win that would make the Spartans believe that this year from hell might not have been completely without value. That win felt like a foundational piece for the program Michigan State can be under Mel. Did it mean the Spartans could beat superpower Ohio State the following week? Hell no. They lost 52–12. But Ohio State was headed to a Big Ten title, a Sugar Bowl win, and a spot in the national title game. (And Northwestern would give Ohio State more trouble in the Big Ten title game than it gave Michigan State.)

No one expected the Spartans to be capable of winning the Big Ten in Mel's first year. But if they'd followed that blowout loss to Indiana by laying down against Northwestern, then there would have been a lot of questions about whether Mel was the guy to lead the Spartans back to glory. But he downshifted to neutral. He chose the next right step. And he proved brighter days are ahead as long as the Spartans trust the process.

# CHAPTER 4

# DETERMINING YOUR VALUES

Russell Wilson spent most of his NFL career known as a guy who didn't deliver strong opinions. This was calculated on his part. His success on the field spoke for him.

But in the summer of 2020, Russell decided he couldn't stay quiet. As protests raged across the country following the death of George Floyd while in the custody of Minneapolis police, Russell realized he had something he needed to say. So he wrote a letter that he posted on his social media channels expressing his anger and fear. He couldn't believe that in the twenty-first century, he had some of the same concerns for his children that his grandmother had for hers two generations earlier. "I fear for their lives just like my grandmother feared for my dad's life and the lives of her other children," Russell wrote. "I fear because of the color of their beautiful chocolate skin."[1]

Shortly after that, Russell held a press conference to explain himself further. He answered questions about his childhood in Richmond, Virginia, where his father—an Ivy League–educated attorney—taught him to keep his hands out of his pockets at gas stations so he wouldn't be accused of stealing. At the time, Russell never thought he'd have to offer similar lessons to his kids, but he told the reporters on the Zoom call that he'd learned he'd need to do that even before he had children. Russell learned that five years earlier at a dining room in Southern California.

It was early in 2015. Russell and the Seahawks had lost to the Patriots in Super Bowl XLIX only a few weeks earlier. Russell had set up shop in SoCal to train in order to try to bring Seattle back to the Super Bowl for a third consecutive season. I helped him choose the location, and it seemed like a perfectly nice place. One morning, we were eating breakfast at a restaurant near the house Russell had rented. The area was overwhelmingly older and white, but we hadn't thought anything of it. This was 2015 in California, not 1952 in Alabama. But as Russell waited in line for his turn at the buffet that morning, an older white man behind him said, "That's not for you." Initially, we thought the guy was joking. Maybe he was a 49ers fan who wanted to rib a player on a rival team. But within seconds, it became clear he wasn't kidding. This really was a white man in 2015 telling a Black man that he didn't belong in the same dining room. Russell ignored the guy, got his food, and returned to the table.

There were three of us there, and we all simmered in silence. No one knew what to say. We couldn't believe what had just happened. We couldn't believe anyone would say that in twenty-first century America. Russell finally couldn't take it anymore. He got up from the table and walked over to the man.

"I don't appreciate you talking to me that way," Russell said. "I have as much right to be here as you do."

I'm not naming the place because the management—which certainly didn't support that man's views—handled the incident quickly and professionally. But the incident shook Russell. It also shook me. I didn't know what to tell him. Unfortunately, it brought Russell right back to all those lessons his father had taught him as a child. It reinforced that we hadn't come that far. "That was a heavy moment to me," Russell said in that 2020 press conference. "This is really still real."

Russell didn't mention the incident publicly until that 2020 press conference. Why did he do it then? Because he wanted to live in line with his values. Russell wants a world where his children never have to experience that kind of intolerance. That's critically important to him. So he chose to speak up even though he'd publicly stayed largely silent on nonfootball matters. "I'm praying that my kids don't have to grow up in a world where they have to face that much weight every day when they walk outside," he said.

We all need to make sure we live in line with our own values because that's the only way to truly stay neutral. If we're out of alignment, our decisions and our behaviors won't feel correct in our minds. They won't help us reach our goals. Values provide the foundation for living neutrally. Values are what we prioritize at a given moment in our lives based upon a lifetime of information we've acquired. They become our own baseline either consciously or subconsciously. There are no "correct" values, despite people hoping to ascribe them onto us. They live within us and steer our decisions. They could be wealth, health, spirituality, faith, family, success, greed, or growth. They change with our socialization, but largely, once formed, they drive our decisions now and into the future. They are, essentially, what we believe matters.

Values are critical to neutral behavior because they've already guided our past and current behavior whether we know it or not. They drive what we do and ultimately who we become. They are not right or wrong. They simply are. It's a little scary when you think about it. Neuroscientist Joe Dispenza explains that it's critical for us to become conscious of our values or life becomes a series of "repetitive actions"—literally Groundhog Day. The same values drive the same thoughts which drive the same decisions which drive the same actions which produce the same outcomes. We can break this cycle by modifying our behavior, but we need to know what drives us.

I grew up a fairly privileged kid, so it wasn't until 1994 that I experienced my first real adversity. In my freshman year of college, I got shingles. That led to immune-system challenges, to dropping out of college temporarily, to ulcerative colitis— which may have laid some of the groundwork for the medical issues I've dealt with since 2019—and ultimately to a summer of forced deep thinking.

I'd been living a happy-go-lucky existence to that point. I certainly had allowed my values to subconsciously run my life on autopilot. But all the thinking that summer forced me to grab control and do an audit of how and why I got there. I needed to control what would happen next by changing the trajectory I'd fallen into. Twenty-five years later, on that September day in 2019, I felt exactly the same.

After addressing the health issues medically and learning I'd need to sit out a full year of soccer and basketball, I knew I was on the right path relative to medication and physical well-being. The next plan would address my psychological well-being. Dad put a Post-it note in my window after my first colonoscopy that said, "If it is to be, it's up to me." I agreed. No one can influence my future like I can. I was grateful to be raised with these principles so deeply embedded in me at a very young age. I built out a plan that could get me critical answers to questions that my first year of college had raised within me. (This is what college is designed to do if your values aren't clearly entrenched.) I needed to decide what mattered to me.

Why do I go to church? What do I believe in? Why do I practice abstinence at nineteen years old? Why am I not remotely driven academically even though I want to graduate? What really is important to me? I really had no idea what these answers were anymore. I needed to examine all of it, and I did

my most thorough examination, oddly enough, while working
at a basketball camp.

My initial plan was to sustain a high level physically so that
when I returned to college sports I'd be ready, and NBC
camps were the answer. NBC had a dual meaning—Northwest
Basketball Camps and Northwest Bible Camps. The camps
brought in players from across the Pacific Northwest, and they
drew dozens of male and female NCAA and NAIA college
players to serve as councilors. The goals for the councilors—of
which I'd be one—were to stay on their game while on summer
break, help others, and explore their Christian faith. Many
players went with college teammates or friends they played
AAU ball with during high school. I got to my first three-week
series of camps in Idaho literally knowing no one outside
of Central Washington University's head men's coach Gil
Coleman, who was friends with my dad and who had watched
me grow up in his camps.

The camps were a jolt to my comfort zone. I'd worked camps
before, but nothing like this. Our growth as basketball players
and as Christians were equally prioritized. We had required
Bible study every morning from 6 to 7. Then we prepared the
facilities. Then we spent hours coaching basketball drills. After
that came evening fellowship, testimonials, and dinner. Dessert
consisted of intense pickup basketball games.

As a Catholic, I didn't bring a Bible. I had one, but our faith
is very private. While I was competent, I was nothing like the
people in this group. Their knowledge of scripture and their

comfort speaking openly about it blew my mind. The first week, I just sat and listened. I felt a bit exposed and very much different.

The basketball was a blast, and I met amazing people like Fresno State guard Brandon Bakke, and did skits for all the kids at night. I fit in socially and athletically, but the questions about what I valued kept multiplying. One of the discussions led by Shann Ferch hit me square between the eyes. Shann was a high school legend in Montana who started his college career at Montana State and then transferred to Pepperdine. He went on to play professionally in Germany and now serves as a professor of leadership studies at Gonzaga University in Spokane, Washington. Shann has written novels and collections of poetry. He edits a scholarly journal. He's truly an amazing person, and he probably does not remember meeting me at that camp. But I absolutely remember him.

During one of those discussions at camp, Shann talked about "playing on fire for the Lord." That—good or bad—for him, it was about God. Shann could flush the adversity or the success of the game because he knew there was a purpose far bigger than him. He found those answers in the Bible. I had no comprehension of what he was talking about. I had never connected my faith as a verb. I had prayed countless times before or after games, but my faith had never been a part of the game.

When I watched Shann, I so badly wanted what he had. The emotional toll basketball had taken on me in college was brutal.

I was terrified before every game. I was terrified during every game. Risk aversion led to hesitancy on the court. He had none of that. He was much better than me at basketball, but it wasn't his skill that separated us. It was his faith.

After the second week of camp, I pulled him aside after a pickup game and he made some time for me. I asked how he did it. He said it was submission. He'd given up the external benefits or consequences of the game. I wanted to do that. And I tried. I loved those Bible studies at the camp and, after each one, I walked out rejuvenated. But within hours the feeling would fade. I tried "playing for the Lord," like Shann, but inevitably I crashed a few days into it.

The one thing I was able to complete at Occidental before that summer was an intense independent study on Malcolm X. The respect I built for him and his evolution and leadership still moves me to this day. I watched his speeches and was moved by his journey. I didn't expect my independent study class to intersect with my Christian basketball camp, but it did. I was in my sixth and final week at the NBC Camps—this time in Spokane. In one of the morning Bible studies, the discussion leader explained that people who didn't accept basic tenets of Christian faith could never go to heaven. I grabbed a youth minister I'd gotten to know during the camps. We talked about Malcolm X, and the minister acknowledged how vital Malcolm was to the American fabric. But he also explained that Malcolm couldn't have gone to heaven. I was stunned. That made no sense to me.

I went on later that summer to take courses at school on Buddhism, Taoism, and Western Asian religions. The more educated I got, the more confused I was. I finally found some clarity during a visit home before my junior year. As if by magic—or perhaps by providence—I bumped into my youth minister. He was a former soccer player at Santa Clara University and an all-around badass. He was one of the few people with whom I was comfortable sharing my journey of the previous few months. So as we shot baskets one day, I told him about the camps, about trying and failing to play on fire for the Lord. I told him about Malcolm X and heaven. I told him about studying the other religions at college. And I admitted I was more confused than ever about what I believed. How was that even possible? I had no regrets, but I also still had no answers for the questions I posed for myself. I couldn't seem to be like the others I met at the camps. I truly envied them. They seemed so sure. I was so grateful to be engaged with so many peers who seemed to have many more answers about what was important and foundational to them then I did. But I still wanted to find those answers for myself. He stopped bouncing the ball and looked me in the eye and said one of the most profound things I'd ever been told.

"Life is in the questions, Trev," he said. "You were right to ask them. It took trauma to get you to ask them, but you were right."

I nodded my head, frozen in the moment.

"This is the truth. Every answer to every question I seek lies in the Bible for me. Every one," he said. "That just simply isn't the truth for you. Now you know for sure. And what you learn about you is everything in this world. None of the great schools you've been part of or are attending can give you that education."

I nodded again.

"The truth is to find out the individual values that are important to you and live your life in adherence with them," he said. "This creates alignment. This creates congruency. This assures that you are on the path you set and makes your foundation strong. Even your health breaking down may not be able to keep you from your vision and goals."

That was it.

It was a seminal moment in my life that was born out of shitty circumstances. It led to better behavior, to winning behavior. That's the kind of behavior we're exploring in this book. Greatness and failure lived within that same moment. For a college-age Shann Ferch playing Division I basketball, it was total submission. That allowed him to forget the pressure of winning or losing because he was playing for a different reason. That didn't work for me, but I needed to know that so I could seek out what did work for me.

By the end of the summer, I knew my values. I knew what mattered to me. Academic success mattered. Athletic work rate—not necessarily athletic success—mattered. Being well-rounded mattered. My spirituality mattered. Having good, force-multiplying people in my life mattered. What does that mean? It means a person whose qualities enhance your own instead of leeching off them. Shann knew what worked for him and, through trial and error, I had figured out what worked for me.

My world got much bigger after that experience. I was now on much more solid footing for whatever would come my way—good or bad—and my college experience going forward was significantly improved because I examined those values every single day. More importantly, I learned how to live them.

Values shape the pillars of identity, not just for individuals but for teams, units, companies, and entire countries. They might include our religious faith, but they also are the secular version of our faith. They define our trust in why we do what we do. When that identity gets challenged, it can be very unsettling. How do we manage? Not everyone can. As a college student, I couldn't until I took a hard look and reestablished my own values.

One of the most common examples of this is when our money is critical to who we are and then we experience financial hardship. Who are we then? Though most people won't admit it, almost all of us wrap some of our identity in our income level. The truly happiest people don't, but that's not the easiest place to reach. This is why neutral, nonjudgmental, nonbiased values become a game changer because we can evaluate them through the proper lens. Health was and still is a huge value for me. How I exercised, ate, and played sports mattered when I was younger. As I aged, I replaced the competitive sports with regular exercise. As I dealt with surgeries, chemotherapy, and radiation treatment in 2019 and 2020, I couldn't exercise the way I wanted. For a while, I felt lost. A part of me that mattered had been taken away, so I had to adjust my values. In this case, "health" didn't always mean running or hiking or doing yoga. It meant sitting still so I didn't pop a stitch and have fluid draining out of me.

How do you manage when those things are taken away from you in the short term? Are you not who you thought you were? Unfortunately, some people can't adjust.

I was jolted in middle school when my father shared a story about a friend of his in a local town. He shared this later with the masses in seminars and in a powerful video series he made in the 1990s called *Unlocking Your Potential*. This story was about a star quarterback who fit every stereotype of the model high school "stud." His letterman's jacket displayed patches for football, basketball, and track. Great looking young man. Smart, beautiful girlfriend. From the outside, he was who many of us once aspired to be. But unbeknownst to the outside world, his identity was far too dependent on his relationship with his girlfriend.

She was a freshman and he was a junior. He was crazy about her. They spent most of their free moments together his junior year and the summer between his junior and senior years. As his senior football season approached, she realized he'd be going on to college soon and she would still have two more years in high school. She wanted to manage the transition well, so she sat him down for what she believed was a responsible conversation.

"Dave, you know how much I care for you, don't you?" she asked.

"Of course I do," he said. "And, Lisa, I absolutely feel the same way about you."

"I've been doing a lot of thinking this summer," she said. "You're a senior now with an incredible future. You've got college and a football career ahead of you."

"If all goes well," he said. "But I'm not sure what you're saying, Lisa."

"Well, I love you as much as any high school sophomore can love someone, but I really think for your final year and my sophomore year I'd like us to just be friends," she said. "I have so much to learn about myself. And you have so many great experiences to look forward to as a senior. I really think this is what I want us to do."

He was stunned. "Is there someone else?" he asked. "I don't understand at all."

"There's no one else, Dave," she said. "No one."

"I don't get it," he said. "Did I do something wrong?"

"No, of course you didn't," she said. "This is what I believe we should do. It's that simple."

"Well I can't live without you, Lisa!" he yelled. Then he stormed off to football practice.

She thought she knew him. He seemed so stable on the field, in class, and in life. So she didn't take those words too seriously. She hated to see him disappointed, but she believed it was in their best interests. She figured, like many seniors, he'd soon get excited for his newfound freedom. But what she didn't understand was how critical she'd become to who he thought he was. His values were out of whack. Despite all he had going for him, Dave thought that the entirety of his existence hinged on being her boyfriend.

Later that night, Lisa was doing homework when the phone rang.

"Hello," she said.

It was Dave. "Lisa, did you really mean what you talked about earlier today?" he asked. It seemed to have settled upon him that he really might be losing her.

"Yes, Dave," she said. "You know how much I care about you. I've thought long and hard about this, and I believe this really is best for both of us. I know you'll see that too."

"No I won't, Lisa," he said. "I won't, and I just don't see a path forward."

"What are you talking about?" she said.

"Look out your window in an hour and you'll see me hanging from your tree," he said. Before she could respond, he hung up.

Lisa was stunned. She'd had such a great relationship with the school's most solid guy. How could he be saying these things? They sounded so different from the Dave she saw every day. She was upset, but she didn't call anyone. She just knew he wasn't serious. But as she studied, she kept an eye on the clock. When the phone rang an hour later, Lisa was staring out her window.

It was Dave. "Lisa?" he said.

"Yes," she said.

"Did you look?" he asked.

"What are you doing?" she yelled. "Why are you doing this?"

"Look out your window in an hour," he said. "And this time you'll see me hanging from your tree." Again, he hung up before she could respond.

Another hour went by. As she looked out the window, the phone rang.

It was Dave again. "Lisa, did you look?" he asked.

"Dave, you've got to stop this," she said. "After all we've been through, I know this isn't you."

"It is me, Lisa," he said quietly. "Look out in an hour and I can promise you I will be hanging from that tree."

"Dave—don't do thi . . ."

He hung up again.

Lisa couldn't believe this was how their relationship would end. She decided to stop indulging Dave. An hour came, and she refused to look. The phone didn't ring. Sixty-five minutes. Then seventy. No call. Finally, she ran to the window and slid open the shades. There was Dave, hanging with his letterman jacket on. She sprinted down the stairs screaming. Her father ran out and cut Dave down immediately, but it was too late. He slipped into a coma and died the next day.

How can this happen? (And it does happen. Far too often.) It happens to the student who gets a B. To the star athlete. To the CEO who loses her job. It happens to those who, from the outside, have everything going for them and then snap when something goes wrong. Many times, these people value one particular facet of their identity so much that they can't function when that piece is taken away or harmed. They get so wrapped up in one part of themselves that they lose sight of everything else.

We are often guided by what we believe to be true, and that doesn't always match what actually is true. From the outside, delusion is clearly fiction. But inside that person's mind, delusion feels like reality. In politics a few years back, the world was flooded with the idea of *alternative facts*. What the heck are those?

There are either facts or lies. But our minds can create unique alternative facts if we're not constantly examining our values to ensure we keep a healthy balance. Getting ourselves to neutral can be an antidote. Neutral thinking simply doesn't allow for self-inflicted alternative beliefs to exist for long periods.

Seahawks coach Pete Carroll, and many of the coaches who have worked for him, embrace a concept called "Tell the Truth Monday." This is the day the coaches and players come together to watch their last game. No matter how a player thinks he performed, the cameras that filmed the game will give him an unbiased look. The lineman who thought his teammate missed an assignment and cost the team a sack may learn that it was actually he who missed the assignment. The receiver who sulked because he went without a catch may learn that he made a successful block that made all the difference in the play that produced the game-winning touchdown. Ballet dancers and boxers, meanwhile, use mirrors while they practice to gather unbiased, real-time information. The mirrors don't lie to them, and that makes it impossible to lie to themselves if their technique isn't perfect. If we bombard ourselves with facts, our delusions get buried.

Knowing what you value, trust, and prioritize helps you collect facts and avoid delusions. If you value your fitness, you can count how many times you've exercised in the past few weeks. If that number is low, then you'd only be lying to yourself if you believed you were meeting your fitness goals. If you value spending time with your children, then you can catalogue exactly when you took advantage of opportunities for quality time and when you blew them off to watch TV. Collect these facts.

Count them up. Neutral thinking won't let you lie to yourself. It will tell you if you're living in line with your values or if you're falling out of alignment. If you are, it's up to you to do a self-assessment. Ask yourself, "What truly matters to me?" Once you've determined that, do an inventory of what you've done to live your values. That way, you can adjust your goals and your habits. All of this is connected. Our values are what we consider the cornerstones of ourselves. We set goals to make sure we live up to our values. We form habits to ensure we reach our goals. When all of these align, we succeed. When we fail, we can examine our values, goals, and habits to determine where along the line we faltered. Then we can fix the issue because we have all that information and we understand how to use it.

Just as important as your own personal values are your organization's values. This matters in a few different ways. First and foremost, we all instinctively crave being part of a group that shares our values and helps us live in line with them. Whether that's a place of business, a school for our children, a religious congregation, or a social organization, we want what matters most to us to matter to the people with whom we choose to associate. Meanwhile, when we have children, we want to make sure they grow up with a strong set of values that they know and understand clearly. Back at work, those of us who do manage others must establish a strong set of values to help the people under us thrive.

One of the best examples I've seen of this in my career is Nick Saban's building of the architecture of the football program at Alabama. Nick brought me and several other consultants in when he got hired in 2007. Our job was to help him establish a winning culture that could sustain itself. Nick had done this previously at LSU, so he knew what he wanted it to look like. But the program needed work. After all, there were plenty of reasons the previous staff got fired.

Nick created a work environment where each staffer in the organization understood exactly what was expected. That way, Nick knew each employee had been educated as to what their job actually was when Nick invoked the "do your job" mantra he'd learned working for Bill Belichick. Nick also wanted to lay out a set of program values for the players so they understood what produced consistent success.

The Crimson Tide went 7–6 in Nick's first year, and some of it was ugly. The low point on the field was a 21–14 loss in November to Louisiana-Monroe, a massive underdog that didn't have near the resources or talent of Alabama. The off-field low point in the off-season that followed came when a player inherited from the previous regime was arrested and later convicted of selling cocaine. He had even been spotted selling drugs in the parking lot of Alabama's football facility.

Nick wanted to change the program so it had a foundational set of values in order to ensure that players knew the team would be able to succeed. The freshmen in 2008 would be the first group entirely recruited by Nick to Alabama, and that group— which included future NFL stars Julio Jones, Dont'a Hightower, and Mark Ingram—would go on to set a standard that helped create one of college football's ultimate dynasties. One of the

first things that group and Alabama's veteran players received
when they arrived to prepare for the 2008 season was a mental-
skills manual that I had written to help codify many of Nick's
philosophies. The table of contents reads like a list of values
that any organization should strive to nurture:

*Perseverance*

*Work Ethic*

*Teamwork*

*Individual Responsibility to the Team*

*Dominance*

*Thriving with Pressure*

Later, we included more concrete concepts that also could be
defined as program values. These veered more toward the habits
we hoped the players could develop to live aligned with the more
abstract values. The concepts on this list also mattered deeply to the
head coach, and they would come to matter deeply to the players:

*Relaxation*

*Sleep*

*Time Management*

Very little of this had been emphasized by the old regime. Some of the more basic concepts (perseverance, work ethic, teamwork) had been addressed by every coach these players had ever had, but they hadn't been constantly reinforced. They certainly didn't get seventeen suggestions for better sleep in their mental-skills manual. Here are some examples:

- *If you aren't asleep after twenty minutes, get out of bed. Find something else to do that will relax you. If you can, do this in another room and then go back to the bedroom when you are sleepy. Avoid activities that alert your mind (video games, exercise, exciting TV programs, etc.) and bright light.*

- *Avoid going to bed hungry, but don't eat a big meal near bedtime either. Milk, peanuts (peanut butter), yogurt, ice cream, and turkey are good snacks to help you relax. Have a glass of warm milk or a slice of toast with peanut butter. Avoid spicy foods before bedtime.*

- *Think of peaceful, relaxing, and calm places and thoughts as you lie down. Remember times when you were most relaxed. Think of your favorite place to be that is relaxing and allow your breathing to be relaxed and consistent.*

Does any of that help beat LSU or Auburn? It absolutely does. All of it helps, in fact. Every detail matters, and Nick did a fantastic job of making sure players knew what the program valued and how to set goals and form habits to live up to those values.

After getting substantive time with some incredible experts
to focus specifically on the mentality and formation of the
emerging "'Bama Way," I spoke to the team early in the 2008
preseason camp. I reiterated much of what we hit on in the
summer and helped set the tone for an incredibly important
season. A strong camp was the next step as we prepared to face
favored Clemson in the season opener.

I can't begin to explain how grateful I was for the trust Nick
placed in me. Time is so valuable in a football program. When
my former partner Chad Bohling and I worked with the
Jacksonville Jaguars around the turn of the century, coach Tom
Coughlin held meetings that started on the half-a-minute.
(For instance, you have from 8:35 and 30 seconds until 8:40
and 30 seconds to make your presentation.) If Chad and I
were presenting, you couldn't get in the team room until
the second your time began. The trust coach Saban showed
to make time during the summer for consultants like myself
to specifically educate the players on the fundamentals of
thinking was incredible. It helped us create meaningful change.
In my presentation, I reminded the players that knowing
what mattered to them is the first step. We couldn't force the
coaching staff's values down their throats, but we could explain
why a strong value system mattered and let them help design
one that worked for themselves.

The most satisfying part of working with Alabama was
watching the players discover what they valued and then
seeing them create a culture that didn't necessarily have to
be dictated by the coaches. That 2008 team beat Clemson in

its first game and went on to win its first twelve games. The next year, the Crimson Tide won the program's first national title since 1992. By my last year at Alabama in 2015, it was the older players—not the coaches—who usually explained the program's values to the younger ones. The veterans enforced the value system and made sure everyone lived up to it. That 2015 team won the national title in large part because everyone in the organization pulled in the same direction because of their shared values.

In the summer of 2019, I had the honor of presenting some of the mental-skills manuals that I'd made for various teams to Kobe Bryant at his Mamba Academy in Thousand Oaks, California. I explained the mental architecture I helped create for those teams, and Kobe listened intently. One of the best parts I took from my conversation with him was this: "I think what's key when you're doing what you do with these players is that you want them to get to the natural conclusions you'd hope for—not to force them there," Kobe said. "As a team is forming its identity, a lot of opinions may need to be heard. Some guys have reasons why social media during the season is good. Or less practice time is better. That may not make sense, but you want them to work through that together."

And that is a critical factor to consider if you manage others. Just because something matters to you doesn't necessarily mean it will matter as much to the people you manage. Lay out what matters most to the organization, and then help the employees build a value system within that architecture that allows them to feel invested as well. Then, like that 2015 Alabama team, everyone will want to stay in line with the values they've helped create.

This process of alignment works in any area you wish to focus on, whether it's sports or home life or business. I've been working with Christian Nowakowski, an entrepreneur who is expanding his business. Christian found success as an individual investor, but as time passed, he realized he wanted to launch an investment firm that could operate at a larger scale. He started by examining his personal values to see how they would line up with the values of his company.

First, Christian values maximizing his potential. He doesn't just want to be good. He wants to be the best he can possibly be. He felt the same way as a young hockey player and golfer, and he eventually reached his potential in those sports. Like most of us, that wasn't good enough to make the pros. "I'm not in the NHL," he says. "I'm not on the PGA Tour." (But he did become a scratch golfer, which is a lot better than most.)

As he expands and brings employees into the fold, Christian would like to imbue the entire company with the mindset of always trying to maximize. Working in line with this value requires constant evaluation and stress-testing. It requires employees to continuously ask, "How can we be better?"

Secondly, he values growth. He never wanted to allow himself to stagnate. This was a good reason for him to pursue

expansion. Had continued growth not been so important
to him, Christian might have been better off remaining an
individual investor. But new challenges matter to him. They
keep him focused. Wanting to grow allowed Christian to set
goals that helped him create habits that can make the company
better in the long run.

Lastly, Christian was a bulldog at work, but he didn't turn
that off when he went to the gym after work. So he has set
out to look for people with similar mindsets to populate the
company.

When his personal and organizational values didn't completely
align, he avoided putting them in direct conflict by adjusting
his habits. "If you value family time but you're trying to make
many millions of dollars, those values might not always line
up," he says. But that doesn't mean Christian can't enjoy family
time *and* make millions of dollars. He realized that since both
of those things matter to him, he needed to make adjustments
elsewhere. If you want to work your ass off and spend time
with your family, then the bulk of your free time must be spent
with your family. Values helped create priorities which helped
create a change in habit that allowed for living in line with both
values. "There is no right or wrong answer," Christian says. "It's
just what you want out of life."

When we take on a new challenge (expanding a business) or
get a challenge thrown at us (the C-word, getting laid off),
it can make us question exactly who we are. These questions

hit especially hard when we didn't choose the challenge. The truth? We are exactly the same person we were before—except we were benched, fired, diagnosed, dumped. Positive thinking struggles to offer many of us consolation in such moments. Negative thinking embitters us. Its power makes us believe that this may be a trend that will redefine who we are going forward—that it's a snowball headed down a mountain that is going to turn into an avalanche.

Staying neutral gives us a fighting chance. Building out neutral values gives us a solid base that allows us to own the adversity when it comes—and it will—but not to be defined by it. The term *owning it* may have grown in popularity as an idiom in recent years, but it shouldn't be a linguistic fad. It means you take responsibility. It means you have the accountability to acknowledge that your current reality is very much happening and has consequences, but it also allows for a new reality based on your next step after facing today's challenge. In these moments, there are few answers to make them better. Stepping back after losses—either in sports or in life—is critical. A football team watches the tape. So can you. My C-word diagnosis was, in many ways, crushing for me, but limiting who I called and avoiding doom-scrolling on the internet helped me manage the immediate mental chaos. It allowed me to not make it worse. It allowed me time to get my mind around the plan going forward, manage my own thinking, and stay in alignment with my values.

Values can be anchors for us in the moment. They are the things we prioritize. By remembering what matters to us and making decisions that help us stay in alignment with those concepts, we can get back to neutral.

So what are your values? Let's try an exercise I use with my clients to help them identify what really matters to them.

My youth minister did a version of this verbally. My father codified it into an activity he used for high-functioning corporate clients. For my minister, it basically was "find out what's important to you and live your life in alignment with that." Because of the journey I'd been on, it resonated.

My father's version, at the simplest level, is an alignment assessment, and all you need is a note card. Draw a line down the middle of the front of the card. On the left half, write "Five Values" at the top and then number one through five down the left. On the right half, write "Five Goals" at the top and then number one through five. On top of the left half of the back, write "Current Behavior" and number one through five. On top of the right half, write "Ideal Behavior."

The idea is simple. The things that are important to you on the left front and the long- or short-term goals on the right front should be connected.

If time with family is a value, then a goal could be to stop working so much on the weekends or to spend less time in the evenings browsing Instagram and more time being engaged with your family. Or, if you don't yet have a family, the goal could be to build one.

If you value hard work, your goal might be to achieve a better career. Maybe you have in mind a specific job title within your current company, or you could think bigger and set your goal as being at the top of your industry.

Many times what I see is a list of values and goals that don't align. We see this frequently with young people. (Young Trevor earlier in this chapter is a great example.) Their goals might be a list of things their parents wish they could do. They match mom and dad's values, but they might not match that person's values at all, so the young person's behaviors don't match their goals. One of the most difficult parts of becoming an adult is realizing that you and your parents may not value exactly the same things. Life becomes easier and more fulfilling when you step back and examine what truly matters to *you*.

You're not necessarily wrong when your values don't match your goals. It only means you either need to change your goals to better fit your values or take a deeper look at what you define as important. It's probably best to start with the values themselves because accurate values should help create more attainable goals. To do that, you have to be brutally honest with yourself.

Values and goals can change over time. I've been with some of the best athletes and coaches who had audacious goals matched to their values. But four or five years down the road, these people hadn't realized how much success or adversity had changed their values. Now their goals didn't match up.

Often, success creates new or different adversity and this is where the back page becomes key. Objectively define how you currently behave and develop that into how you should ideally behave to achieve your goals in alignment with your values. This is where the Illusion of Choice concept that I covered in *It Takes What It Takes* rings most true. You always have a wide array of options, but to get what you want, you usually have very few actual choices. Christian's example is a great one. He wants to spend time with his family. He wants to make millions of dollars for his company. So when his buddies call and say they're taking the boat out Saturday, he doesn't really have a choice if he wants to accomplish both his goals. He's going to say no thanks and stay home with the family.

I use this exercise to show people that "wanting" is not enough. Your values will always drive what you're able to accomplish because they will dictate your behaviors. If you truly value rest, you're not going to go out drinking until 3 a.m. You're going to brew yourself a cup of tea, read a book, and get to sleep by 11 p.m.

But even world-class athletes and successful businesspeople can fall out of alignment. It happens to everyone.

The alignment fades because our values have changed slightly. Maybe being "the absolute best" as a football or basketball player has been replaced by family or entrepreneurship or options that weren't available to the player when they originally formulated their values. That's why we have to

reexamine what matters to us every once in a while. Start
with a fresh note card. List it out again. If the priority list has
changed, so will the goals and the behaviors. If you think
the priorities are the same, then ask why the behaviors are
different. Do you need to adjust what you value? Or do you
need to adjust your behavior?

# CHAPTER 5

# BEHAVING YOUR WAY TO SUCCESS

In 2014, the University of Texas invited an alumnus to address a graduating class of more than 8,000. That alumnus was Navy Admiral William McRaven, future chancellor of the University of Texas system and then the commander of US Special Operations Command. At the time, McRaven was the longest serving Navy SEAL. Three years earlier, he had been in charge of Operation Neptune Spear, better known as the raid that killed Osama bin Laden.

McRaven built his commencement speech around one of the school's mottos: "What starts here changes the world." He explained to the graduates ten lessons he learned in SEAL training that would help them change the world. The first lesson?

*Make your bed.*[1]

The crowd of new graduates laughed, thinking he was joking. He wasn't. When McRaven was in SEAL training in 1977, his instructors came in every morning to inspect his bed. The corners were expected to be square. The covers were expected to be pulled tight. The pillow was to be centered under the headboard, and the extra blanket was to be folded and stored at the foot.

"If you make your bed every morning, you will have accomplished the first task of the day," McRaven told the graduates. "It will give you a small sense of pride, and it will encourage you to do another task and another and another. By the end of the day, that one task completed will have turned into many tasks completed. Making your bed will also reinforce the fact that little things in life matter. If you can't do the little things right, you will never do the big things right."

Then McRaven allowed himself a tiny smile.

"And, if by chance you have a miserable day, you will come home to a bed that is made—that you made," he said. "And a made bed gives you encouragement that tomorrow will be better."

I sent that simple, powerful message to Russell Wilson in the spring of 2021. The rest of McRaven's advice is excellent, but that first piece explains more beautifully than anything I've ever heard one of the most valuable pieces of living neutrally: first you form your habits, then they form you.

Once you've catalogued your values and you know what matters to you, you can examine your habits. If you believe you value fitness and yet your habits don't include regular exercise, do you really value fitness? Or do you need to change your habits so they align with your values?

Determining your values is talking the talk; your habits are how you walk the walk. They are what you do every day to ensure you get what you want. Or they're what you do every day to ensure you *don't* get what you want. They are the choices you make again and again that lead to success or failure.

Living neutrally isn't a philosophy. It's a course of action. So it requires action. It requires you to decide you want to embrace the behaviors that allow you to live in line with your values. The hard part is that you have to keep doing it. Day after day. When you downshift to neutral and choose your next right step, you accept the past, but you also accept that it's not predictive of the future. It's great that you made your bed every day for the past three years, but you still have to make your bed today. It's not about what has been done or what might be done. It's about what we do moment to moment.

My dad defined *habit* with an acrostic poem:

> Have
> A
> Ball
> All
> The
> Time

He knew it was misspelled. He didn't care. The message was too good.

The "Have A Ball" part is true in the sense that once you develop great habits and learn to stay faithful to them, your life will get better. Everything will seem easier because you put in the work on the front end. Plus, there is joy in creating an infrastructure of behaviors that can fuel your progress toward a goal. Essentially, you're building your own operating system. (And just like your iPhone, you may have to download a system update every few days as circumstances change around you.) You'll feel satisfaction with each inch of progress you make. And since you're living neutrally, you aren't focused on the end result. You're focused on the process that moves you toward your goal.

The "All The Time" part is what matters most. Your behaviors define who you are in real time. If you want to live your values, to reach your goals, you have to execute the behaviors to match all the time. Not a few hours a day. Not a few days a week. All. The. Time.

As Russell Wilson and I always say, nothing happens by accident. Habits are the actions we take to turn something possible into something probable. Success is launched by your values. It's built by your behaviors. It's sustained by daily action. And Admiral McRaven wasn't kidding. If you're looking for a place to start, making your bed is a great one.

Let's break down his explanation. McRaven said, "You will have accomplished the first task of the day." Yes, Navy SEALs make their bed perfectly every day. But how much of the rest of the population does it? Fifty percent? Thirty percent? Think about how many people you've met who accomplish literally nothing every day. Or the people who may have a productive day and then follow it by wasting their next two. If you start your day by making your bed—this is not a metaphor; I mean just make your freaking bed—then you probably will be ahead of most of the population.

McRaven also said that making your bed will "give you a small sense of pride, and it will encourage you to do another task and another and another." This works both ways. If we build the habits that help us reach our goals, it becomes easier to stack those habits on top of one another. If you make your bed and then you eat a healthy breakfast and then you hit the gym on the way to work, look at all you've accomplished—and the day is still young. This also works in the other direction. If you can't be bothered to make your bed, you're probably more likely to just skip the gym and shovel some doughnuts into your mouth on the way to work.

Go back to that list of values you created at the end of the last chapter. What habits will get you there?

Top performers, of course, have God-given talent. But so do other people. The people who ascend to the highest level usually do so because they're willing to do the basics better than everyone else—again and again and again.

Ichiro Suzuki wrote down what he valued in the sixth grade. Long before he grew into one of the best hitters in the history of baseball, he was a student at Aichi Prefecture Kasugai-gun Toyonari Elementary School in Kasugai, Japan, where he was told to write an essay.

He titled it "My Dream," and in it, he laid out his plans to become one of the best baseball players in the world.[2] My dad, ever the dutiful Mariners fan, kept an English translation of the original document, which lives in the museum Ichiro's parents run in Nagoya, Japan.

"My dream is to become a first-class professional baseball player," young Ichiro wrote. "To make this dream come true, I have to play very well in the National middle and high school baseball leagues, and in order to do so, I need to practice.

"I have been playing baseball since I was three. I spent half a year practicing baseball from three to seven years of age. Since the third grade, I have been doing hard practice on 360 of 365 days; so I can play with my friends only five or six hours a week."

Ichiro went on to write that he wanted to get at least a million yen when he was drafted. He also wanted to make sure he could give free tickets to all the people who helped him along the way. Ichiro knew then what mattered to him and he already was forming the habits that would make him a star in two countries.

In his book *The Meaning of Ichiro*,[3] Robert Whiting writes that Ichiro played catch with his father every day, and after each throwing session, Ichiro would oil his glove. At the age he was when he wrote that essay, Ichiro was hitting about five hundred pitches a day either from another person or from a pitching machine. Whiting also wrote that when Ichiro was in high school, hitting fastballs had gotten so easy for him that his coach had to crank the pitching machine to its highest setting and move it closer to home plate, in effect creating a 93-mph fastball for young Ichiro to hit.

Ichiro was drafted by the Orix Blue Wave out of high school, and he played professionally in Japan for nine years (with 1,278 hits) before he came to the majors as a Seattle Mariner. When Ichiro came to Seattle, he and his wife rented a three-bedroom apartment. Ichiro and his wife took one bedroom. The second was for guests. The third? That's where Ichiro practiced his swing. Had he played in the majors his entire career, Ichiro probably would own the all-time record for hits. Even with the very late start, Ichiro still finished No. 24 on the all-time MLB hits list with 3,089. He's eligible to be elected to the Hall of Fame in 2025, and he's a near lock to get chosen.

Ichiro collected all those hits thanks in part to habits that set him apart from everyone else in the majors. His on-field stretching routine was always longer and more thorough than that of his teammates. Long after the other players had moved on to the batting cages or the field, Ichiro kept pulling on different joints until every muscle in his body was limber. And this came after an elaborate foam-roller stretching session in the locker room.

Before Ichiro came to the plate, he had another elaborate stretching routine in the on-deck circle. He would squat and then rock from side to side. His teammates tried to mimic him during warm-ups, but none could get as low or move as far in either direction. Then he would bend his knees and flex his legs at 90-degree angles, place each hand on the corresponding knee and push down, flexing his shoulders back and forth. After seasons that lasted at least 162 games—longer if his team made the playoffs—he'd take about three days off and then return to the facility to resume his daily batting practice.

With Ichiro, it's sometimes difficult to tell where the habits stopped and the superstitions started. For instance, before each game he played in the majors, he would lay his jersey across his knees and clip stray threads. He kept his bats in a humidor. He told ESPN's Jim Caple that he took care of his equipment the way a chef took care of his knives.[4] But Ichiro had laid out early that he valued being a great baseball player, and specifically, a great hitter. He built his habits around that value. And in a 2018 video produced by MLB.com, he explained why.[5]

"It's necessary to have a natural-born talent to play baseball in this world," he said, through a translator. "However, one more important thing is whether you could try a little harder when faced with your own limits. In reality, you can't make a much greater effort than others, but I feel it's very important to try a bit harder over and over again."

If you ever hear Kirby Smart or Mel Tucker or Russell Wilson talk about the aggregate of marginal gains, this is what they mean. If you can make a tiny improvement over and over and over again, eventually that adds up to a massive improvement. Ichiro tried a bit harder over and over again, and he became exactly what he set out to be.

Have you built habits that will help you become what you want to be? If you'd like to be a chef, do you try to cook a new meal every day? If you want to be a professional writer, do you write every day? If you want to be a great teacher, do you go looking for innovative lessons every day? If you just want to be a more organized person, do you make a to-do list every day?

Some of the actions that lead to success are actually pretty easy to do—once or twice. What makes people successful is the willingness to repeat those great habits day after day. There will be days when you don't feel like making your bed or stretching or cooking or writing or making a to-do list. But you still need to do them because repeating those behaviors will make a better version of you. Lawrence Frank, who has worked with some of the most freakishly dedicated athletes in the world during a long career as an NBA coach and executive, put it really well. "Behaviors really have to supersede your feelings," Lawrence said. "Sometimes you have to behave your way into feeling it versus feeling your way into behaving."

Allen Stein Jr., a performance coach and motivational speaker who came up through the world of basketball, tells a great story about meeting a young Stephen Curry in 2007. Stein was at the first Kobe Bryant Skills Academy. Nike had invited the top twenty high school shooting guards and the top ten college shooting guards. The high school group included future NBA players Demar Derozan, Jrue Holiday, Lance Stephenson, and future Curry teammate Klay Thompson. The college group included Curry, who had just finished his freshman season at Davidson and who remained largely unknown to casual basketball fans. (He changed that in the NCAA Tournament in 2008.) Stein explained in a YouTube video exactly why he knew Curry would be the best player of the group: "It was all because of his work habits," he said.[6]

Stein noticed that before each of the camp's six workouts (spread over three days), Curry would be on the court a half-hour before any of the other players. And he wasn't just taking random jump shots. He was practicing situational shots to simulate what he might need to make in a game. Stein estimated that Curry made between 100 and 150 shots before the workout even began. During the workouts, Stein saw that Curry would correct his own form without help from the coaches, repeating anything he didn't deem perfect. Then, after each workout, Curry wouldn't leave the court until he had swished five consecutive free throws. Notice that Stein didn't say "made" five consecutive free throws. Because if the ball hit the rim and went in, Curry still made himself start over again. All five makes had to be nothing but net.

So the next time you watch Steph Curry make a shot and you ask yourself how he did it, know he was able to do it because he decided long ago that it mattered to him to be one of the greatest shooters of the basketball the world had ever seen, and he built the habits that would help him become exactly that.

If you're reading this book in order, then, after you read the last chapter, you examined what truly matters to you. You wrote those things down. Now you need to ask yourself two more questions:

- What am I doing every day to help me live in alignment with my values?

- What am I doing every day that will keep me from living in alignment with my values?

- Once you've answered those questions, you need to take these next steps.

  ° Do more of the answers to the first question.

  ° Do fewer of the answers to the second question.

  ° For goodness' sake, make your bed.

# CHAPTER 6

# INDIANA TREVOR AND THE SCROLL OF DOOM

Remember the scene in *Indiana Jones and the Temple of Doom* when the cult member stabs a needle in the kryta doll to keep Indy pinned to the conveyor belt that is headed toward a giant, rock-smashing roller?[1] We're all on that conveyor belt right now, and we're headed toward a brain-scrambling fate, except no one is holding us on the belt using a magic doll. We're doing it to ourselves.

Every time we tap our phones to open Facebook or Twitter or Instagram, we inch closer to the giant rolling pin that will splatter our gray matter everywhere. In 2020, Merriam-Webster released a new entry to its *Words We're Watching* blog: doomscrolling.[2]

*Doomscrolling* and its no-smartphone-required cousin *doomsurfing* essentially mean the same thing. A person consumes as much chaotic, negative news as possible, often in a short time. Doomscrolling comes from the fact that users of social media apps can simply flick the screen of their phones with a swipe up or down to make more bad news appear. The terms began to appear frequently in American popular culture in March and April of 2020 as much of the nation shut down during the early days of the COVID-19 pandemic.

Do you know what didn't shut down during those months? The Negativity Industrial Complex. It felt as if there was more negativity than ever in popular media. The reason? There was.

A 2020 study of thousands of pandemic-related news stories by researchers from Dartmouth College and Brown University[3] found that US media sources were overwhelmingly more negative than English-speaking media in other countries and more negative than authors writing in scientific journals. How much more negative? The researchers found that 87 percent of news stories from major US media sources were negative in tone compared to 50 percent of English-language stories from other countries and 64 percent in scientific journals. The story that inspired the project was the coverage of a potential vaccine for COVID-19. In February 2020, the *Oxford Mail* in the United Kingdom reported that a professor and her team at Oxford University's Jenner Institute were already working on a vaccine. The professor, Sarah Gilbert, was confident a vaccine could be produced much more quickly than usual thanks to previous research into a potential vaccine for Middle East Respiratory Syndrome, a different deadly coronavirus that affected the Arabian Peninsula early in the last decade.

This was huge news, especially considering COVID-19 hadn't really affected the United States yet but seemed likely to strike. And it turns out the scientists were right to be optimistic. A COVID-19 vaccine was ready by the end of 2020 and was being administered by early 2021. That is essentially light speed for the development of a vaccine. But US news sources didn't mention this research until late April, and the first story led with a quote from a British health official suggesting the chances of creating a vaccine anytime in 2020 were slim. The researchers also found that positive research findings regarding school reopenings didn't necessarily result in positive stories. Even when the news was good, the stories remained negative.

You might think that the channel/publication that leans in the direction you lean politically didn't engage in this sort of behavior, but you'd be wrong. The researchers found no evidence of a difference in partisan sources. They were just as negative no matter the political bent.

Why do they do this? Because we want it. Remember, most of our news organizations are for-profit. They aren't in the business of giving us what we don't want. If we didn't watch or read or comment, they'd quickly change tone or find another story to pursue. They keep doing this because we keep scrolling and we keep clicking.

This remains terrible for us. In January 2021, the Centers for Disease Control and Prevention (CDC) essentially told Americans that too much pandemic news was dangerous.[4] On a web page full of tips for coping with stress, the CDC advised this: "Take breaks from watching, reading, or listening to news stories, including those on social media. It's good to be informed, but hearing about the pandemic constantly can be upsetting. Consider limiting news to just a couple times a day and disconnecting from phone, TV, and computer screens for a while." The reason for this is simple. Consuming too much negative news can send your anxiety soaring. A 2020 study by German researchers found that the more time their German respondents spent consuming media to get more information about COVID-19, the higher their anxiety symptoms were on average.

This isn't limited to information about the pandemic, though. That was just a worldwide event that provided a controlled variable that allowed researchers to more easily study these factors. If you want bad news right now about anything, you can find it. It's only a few taps away on your phone. My hope is that you'll learn to fight the urge to make those taps more often than not.

Even though my father and I diverged in our teaching methods, the one concept that has remained constant is that negativity works negatively 100 percent of the time. But my father didn't live to see a day when we would bombard ourselves with so much negativity. He died in 2007. Facebook was only three years old. YouTube was two. Twitter was invented that year.

Instagram, Snapchat, and TikTok weren't even gleams in programmers' eyes.

We have so many pipes to stream negative messages into our brains that we essentially have a waterfall of negativity deluging us at all times—if we let it. This is especially bad because the negatives stick out to us—and stick with us—more than the positives.

This may just be how we're wired. University of Virginia researcher Vanessa LoBue published a study in 2009 in the journal *Developmental Science*[5] that examined how adults and children responded to series of images of happy and angry faces. Previous studies had shown adults detected angry faces more easily than happy ones, and LoBue wanted to see if children responded similarly. So a group of adults and a group of five-year-olds were shown series of images of human faces. Sometimes, they'd be asked to pick the lone happy face out of a group of angry faces. Other times, they'd be asked to pick the lone angry face out of a group of happy faces.

Though the children didn't identify the requested faces as quickly as the adults, they exhibited the same patterns as the adults. Both groups found the angry face among the happy ones the quickest, and both groups took longer to find the happy face among the angry ones.

The previous year, LoBue and fellow UVA researcher Judy S. DeLoache published a paper in the journal *Psychological Science*[6] that described a similar study using snakes and flowers. A group of adults and a group of children between ages three and five were shown sets of photos that contained one image of a snake and multiple images of flowers. They were also shown a set of photos that contained one image of a flower and multiple images of snakes. The adults were faster, but both groups fell into the same patterns. The adults and the children identified the single snake among multiple flowers faster than they identified the single flower among multiple snakes. The researchers explained that the people identified the snakes more quickly because they are "threat-relevant." In other words, the snake is something to worry about. The flower is not.

There are plenty of anecdotal tales to illustrate our propensity to notice—and forever remember—the negative more than the positive or the neutral. Former New York mayor Ed Koch tells the story of riding through New York with then-president Ronald Reagan.[7] The car was crossing 42nd Street amid a throng of well-wishers. Out of all the people cheering, Reagan noticed the person flipping him the bird. "Mr. President, don't be so upset. Thousands are cheering you and only one guy gave you the finger," Koch recalled saying in a column for *Jewish World Review* in 2004. He replied, "That's what Nancy says, that I always see the guy with the finger."

Now imagine the guy flipping the bird is everywhere. He's on your television. He's on your radio. He's on the social media and news apps on your phone. We notice him and we remember him because it's encoded in us to identify potential threats and pay them more attention than the things our minds consider harmless. But it's one thing when we're trying to avoid

running into a grizzly bear while walking back to our caves.
It's quite another when we're bombarded with negative stimuli
everywhere we turn. We remember the posts that made us
mad. We remember the news stories that scared us. Those stick
with us long after the positive has faded. We carry them in our
minds, and they keep gnawing away at us from the inside.

We can choose to unplug and allow our minds to rest. This
doesn't mean we have to be uninformed. It means we need to
be smarter about the inputs to which we expose our brains.

The experiment I detailed in *It Takes What It Takes*—when
I spent a month bombarding myself with sad songs, angry
songs, and cable news—wrecked me. I had to essentially detox
after that. But what I considered torture is just Tuesday for a
lot of people. This especially goes for what the tech industry
calls "digital natives," younger people who grew up with
smartphones in their hands and don't remember a time when
social media didn't exist.

According to the National Center for Health Statistics, the
suicide rate for Americans between the ages of ten and twenty-
four rose 57.4 percent from 2007 to 2018.[8] (That's 6.8 per
100,000 to 10.7 per 100,000.) That study doesn't blame any
particular issue, but it points out that the suicide rate among
that age group remained stable between 2000 and 2007.

Plus, there is plenty of evidence that increased social media
use has led to higher rates of anxiety and depression among
people everywhere. A 2019 study of children aged twelve to

fifteen published in the *Journal of the American Medical Association Psychiatry*[9] found that children who used social media between thirty minutes and three hours a day had an increased risk of mental health issues, and children who used social media at least three hours a day showed a significantly increased risk for mental health issues. A 2018 study published in the *Journal of Social and Clinical Psychology*[10] split undergrad students at the University of Pennsylvania into two groups: one that was allowed ten minutes a day on Facebook, Instagram, and Snapchat, respectively, and one that was allowed to use those platforms as frequently as desired. At the end of the study, the people in the group that was limited to only thirty minutes a day reported feeling less lonely and less depressed.

Social media can be an incredibly useful tool if used properly. It can help you build a brand. It can help you connect with people with similar interests whom you may never have met otherwise. But those benefits have to be weighed against the cost. That cost can be as little as the three minutes of your life you'll never get back after reading a high school classmate's Facebook screed about the last Superman movie he saw. It might be higher.

Have you ever felt like a failure because you're not living the glorious life that your friends seem to be living on Facebook or Instagram? Have you gone on a crash diet because of a comment someone made under a photo of you?

Is it really worth it? I have to use social media to build my business, but if I didn't need to, I don't know if I'd use it at all.

The bad part is not only the direct negativity incurred, like the nasty comments people sometimes make under a photo. The more insidious part is the other situation, where people post fantasies in the hope that their friends will see them and believe they have perfect lives. That friend who looks so put together in every post? That's what they want you to see. The mom whose kids are always perfectly dressed and smiling in every photo? She's not letting you see the mayhem that ensued thirty seconds before the camera clicked. She doesn't want you to see that. She wants you to believe that everything is wonderful and that the sun shines and birds sing every time she walks outside. And you look at that and say, "Why can't my life be like that?"

But here's the secret. Your life probably *is* like that. Because those people fail too. They endure stress. They get fired. They get divorced. They walk out of the house wearing two different socks, but they don't show you that because they want you to believe the illusion they're presenting. They're working hard to mask their own insecurities and, in the process, they're helping create insecurity in you.

There are a few solutions to this. You can keep looking at that stuff with the understanding that it's all an illusion. Know that every perfect Instagram shot probably is surrounded by the same moments of chaos you deal with every day. Or, if your mind refuses to see through the illusion, you can stop looking at it altogether.

In fact, you can treat all of these negative inputs the same way. When I did my experiment in bombarding myself with negativity, I listened to a lot of country music. (Sorry, Sam Hunt.) Maybe country music doesn't bother you one bit. But you know when something is making you mad, making you sad, making you anxious, making you depressed. When you're consuming something that does one of those things and you're consuming it voluntarily, the solution is clear.

Just stop.

Own the obvious. I'm not asking you. I'm telling you. To engage more in this book without accepting this requirement would piss me off!

"What?" you ask. "I'm getting kicked out of a book? What does that mean?" Yes. My goal here isn't to make your book club. The goal is to help and support you. I'm kicking you out of the book if you can't follow this basic direction, because I'm telling you this to help you. Because control matters. My friend Billy Donovan coaches the Chicago Bulls, but before he coached in the NBA, he spent twenty seasons as the coach at the University of Florida. Do you know what he did if his players couldn't follow simple instructions in practice? He kicked them out of the gym. He told them to take a few hours and come back when they were ready to listen.

When you're trying to push yourself to greater heights, every microinch counts. We need to seize them when we can. And we certainly don't need to cede ground because we want to keep reading intentionally slanted news stories that make us mad or scared. Or because we can't stop looking at the Facebook pages of people we haven't talked to since high school. Walking down one path requires a stop by you. I'm not asking for a 180. Just a pause. Get neutral! Now is the time. Let's roll.

I've built my career on doing simple better. So let's make some gains by doing the obvious. I'm not asking you to be mindful, do yoga, or meditate. I'm asking you to stop doing the unnecessary thing that makes you mad/sad/insecure/frustrated/depressed.

If you wait a year to do this, you'll wish you'd started today. So we'll own it. Start today. Just sign this page.

*I, _____ , will own the obvious and the fundamentals of thinking and stop mainlining negativity.*

*Signature _____*

Congratulations. You've agreed to stop competing against yourself. The next time your thumb starts flicking up on that phone, remember that you're Indiana Jones and you're facing a bad guy right out of a Spielberg movie. But you don't need a bullwhip to win. All you need to do is set that phone down and get on with your life.

# CHAPTER 7

# LOCKING ON/LOCKING OUT

High-level professional or college football games really begin with the psychological planning twenty-four to forty-eight hours before the ball gets kicked off the tee. This is when the coaches and the leaders among the players will present a unifying thought to the entire team. When I work with a team, I'm often the one either presenting that thought or teaching the coaches and the leaders how to present it to the team.

At a meeting while Georgia geared up to play Auburn in the 2017 SEC Championship game, players sat down to one such unifying thought on the big screen: STARVE YOUR DISTRACTIONS/FEED YOUR FOCUS.

These players had already spent almost two years learning about neutral thinking. They understood that they shouldn't verbalize negative thoughts. They knew that in stressful situations they should go to the truth and reevaluate. This group had demonstrated an aptitude for nearly everything I teach, but Georgia coach Kirby Smart knew the players were about to play a different kind of game. The stakes were higher. The attention was greater. Nobody else in the SEC was playing that Saturday. It was just Georgia and Auburn with a championship—and a berth in the College Football Playoff—on the line.

Kirby had been through a bunch of these. He was on the staff at Georgia in 2005 when the Bulldogs won the SEC title. While working as Nick Saban's defensive coordinator at Alabama, Kirby had participated in five SEC title games. In those games, Alabama went 4–1. None of Kirby's Georgia players had participated in the SEC's annual extravaganza in Atlanta, so he worried the hoopla surrounding the game might distract the players, who needed to be thinking about the right things at the right time if they wanted to beat an Auburn team that had handed them their only loss of the season—a 40–17 beatdown—only a few weeks earlier.

Kirby asked a few of the players what it meant to starve their distractions and feed their focus. Then he discussed all the things that go on around an SEC Championship game that don't really impact the game but can impact us collectively. TV pundits, family, social media, game tickets. These are all factors players must deal with before regular-season games, but they get cranked up in Atlanta on the first Saturday in December.

The "rat poison," as Nick Saban calls it, gets scattered everywhere.

We all value the ability to focus. It's critical for a neutral thinker. Stephen Covey, the author of *The Seven Habits of Highly Effective People*, wrote that "The main thing is to keep the main thing the main thing." It's simple and true, which is why nearly every football coach I've ever met has said it to his team at one time or another. You may call it "keeping your eyes on the prize," but that isn't a neutral statement because it focuses on the outcome rather than on the process. But the world in the twenty-first century doesn't want us to focus. We've never had more distractions available to us.

The problem is people put pressure on themselves to focus but then go about focusing all wrong. You can't just tell yourself to focus through the cavalcade of distractions on an average day—never mind the day before an SEC title game—and expect yourself to focus. That would be like telling yourself "be neutral" without first removing your negative thoughts and self-talk. We try all sorts of tactics to focus—lights, technology, trigger words, etc. But the most basic and most important step is to stop giving the distractions the nourishment they need to keep distracting us.

When I spoke to that Georgia team, I reminded the players that the mind is like a mobile-phone battery. The more we thumb through our Instagram feeds or play Angry Birds, the less battery we have available when the most important phone call of our lives comes through. The game is the phone call we can't miss. If the battery dies before we can complete the call—or before the phone even rings—then we miss out on the opportunity of a lifetime. So we need to conserve that battery. We can't let the wrong things into our minds, because then we won't be thinking about the right things at the right time.

We must have the discipline to ignore those apps that drain our batteries. Golfer Will Zalatoris took this quite literally while playing in the Masters for the first time in April 2021. At home in Texas, Zalatoris, who didn't even have his PGA Tour card when he qualified for the Masters, played frequently with former Dallas Cowboys quarterback Tony Romo. Romo, who knows quite a bit about distractions after starting at QB for America's Team for ten years, advised the twenty-four-year-old Zalatoris to turn his phone off when the tournament began and leave it off. Zalatoris followed that advice, so he missed much of the mania surrounding his performance. As he headed into the final round one shot off the lead, the internet had made him a meme. The blond, 165-pound Zalatoris bears a striking resemblance to a young Jared Van Snellenberg, who played Adam Sandler's character's caddy in *Happy Gilmore* in 1996. Even Sandler himself chimed in just before Zalatoris teed off that Sunday in Augusta. Sandler tweeted a side-by-side shot of Zalatoris and *Happy Gilmore*'s caddy and wrote, "Have fun today, young man. Mr. Gilmore is watching you and is very proud." Zalatoris didn't see the tweet until after he finished second in the tournament, which earned him $1.2 million and raised his world ranking to the point where he didn't have to worry about qualifying for PGA Tour events for a long time.

When he didn't need to be as focused, Zalatoris powered up his phone again. With no danger of getting distracted from golf shots that could get him paid, Zalatoris finally saw the Sandler tweet. "If you're ever in need of a caddie again, let me know," Zalatoris replied. "I'll be better this time. I'm always available for you, Mr. Gilmore."

Attempting to focus with a phone on is much harder than focusing with a phone off. Pressing that off button is the ultimate neutral statement. Before we can focus on the right things, we must take our attention away from the wrong things. It's also the easier part of the equation. Why? It can still be difficult to keep our minds trained on what matters, but *not* doing something is a discipline available to all of us. We can always turn off the phone or close that app, or ignore the calls from the person who sucks us into their drama. What we let in, we compete against.

Back in 2017, Georgia coaches and players alike repeated the statement, promising to starve their distractions and feed their focus. Position coaches added the concept to the pregame tests they administered to their groups the night before the game. Talented people who are prepared and maximize their bandwidth psychologically have every right to enter a game with confidence. Confidence is earned universally across a wide variety of areas where we have the potential to excel. This isn't bravado for the sake of bravado or positivity with nothing to back it up. These are neutral statements.

*I have prepared thoroughly.*

*I have not allowed myself to get sidetracked.*

*I have focused on the task at hand.*

The person who can say those things absolutely should walk confidently into whatever they're facing.

But distractions can be tricky. When describing how he stayed one of the fastest humans in the world for as long as he did, Olympic sprinter Michael Johnson said identifying something as a distraction could sometimes be a challenge. "The simple fact is that distractions come in many forms—and many that we do not recognize," he said.

There was a guy who predicted the way we'd be distracted years before the methods that distract us now were invented. Michael Goldhaber was a theoretical physicist in the 1980s. He noticed a marked increase in the volume of information available to people. At the time, there was an increase in cable channels and radio stations and magazines. Goldhaber had become intrigued by a phrase credited to a psychologist named Herbert A. Simon: "the attention economy." Basically, we have a finite amount of attention. When we divert it away from something useful, like spending time with our children or cooking a healthy dinner, we don't get that time or mental energy back. This sounds very similar to what I call the *law of substitution*. In my world, this means that your mind can only focus on one prevailing thought at a time. I teach clients that if they recognize they are thinking a negative thought, they need to substitute it with a neutral one.

Goldhaber believed years before anyone else had even thought about it that media companies, advertisers, politicians, and anyone else selling something would have to fight harder than ever to grab that precious prevailing thought in your head. The competition would be fiercer than at any point in our history. In 1997, when many of us had discovered dial-up internet and made our first forays into cyberspace, Goldhaber wrote an essay for *Wired* magazine. He posited that attention would become the currency in the economy developing online.

Among his predictions:

- There would be a new universe of "microstars" who don't achieve movie-star fame but who develop smaller but devoted followings.

These people would have greater power to influence their fans. In our time, your favorite sixth man on your favorite NBA team poses with a new company's sports drink on his Instagram feed. Essentially, Goldhaber predicted the influencer economy fifteen years before it existed.

- The increased demand for our attention will keep us from reflecting, thinking deeply, or enjoying leisure.

How many times have you stared at your phone when you could have been taking a walk or simply relaxing?

- The increased competition for attention will cause us to "shortchange those around us, especially children."

We've all gotten sucked into something on our screen when we should be spending time with our families. If you say you haven't, you're lying.

It's called *paying* attention because there is a cost. At the very least, this is an opportunity cost. Paying attention to one thing keeps you from paying attention to another. And depending on what that other thing is, you can pay a heavy price. Maybe you ignored a golden opportunity for a new relationship because you were glued to your phone. Maybe what you saw on your phone sent you into a negative spiral. Where you direct your focus, you direct your life.

Our mission is to learn first what has distracted us, what is distracting us, and what will distract us. And distractions don't necessarily have to be bad. They also aren't all on the internet—though that's where some of the most common attention traps are. Some distractions are things that slightly alter our original mission. If a sibling calls and sucks you into family drama while you're preparing for a hectic period at work the next day, you know that's a distraction. But what if a cherished friend calls and wants to grab dinner? While that's quite pleasant, if dinner leads to drinks and then to a late night, it also could be a distraction that could keep you from being ready for that pressure-packed day at work. This is when you have to decide what matters more. And it may be that a night with your friend does matter more. Or it may be that you can enjoy some time with that friend, get home by 8 p.m., and have everything ready for work. You have to know yourself well enough to think neutrally—examining all the relevant factors—and make that call. If it veers into distraction, maybe ask if your friend wants to meet up on a different night.

The law of substitution is critical to how our mind works. We can only sustain one dominant thought at a time. When our mind is on that thought, everything is blocked out. My father would teach this as LOCK ON/LOCK OUT. Once we lock on to a thought, everything else gets blocked out. This can be dangerous if we don't understand the difference between or recognize how to identify these two things:

- What we shouldn't focus on.

- What we should focus on.

In your business life, what takes you away from maximizing a workday? In a 2017 survey by CareerBuilder.com,[1] employers listed the following as the biggest drains on productivity.

- Cell phone/texting: 49 percent

- The internet: 38 percent

- Social media: 37 percent

- Gossip: 35 percent

- Email: 29 percent

- Coworkers dropping by: 24 percent

- Smoke breaks or snack breaks: 25 percent

- Meetings: 23 percent

- Noisy coworkers: 19 percent

But it isn't only about nonwork distractions. Sometimes one work project distracts you from another. A 2015 study by an American, a Canadian, and an Italian researcher published in the *Journal of the European Economic Association* examined "task juggling" by Italian judges. Essentially, the judges who tried to juggle more trials at once took longer per case to complete cases than the judges who only worked on a few trials at once. This makes sense. If you have five projects running simultaneously, you probably lose more time shuffling between them than you would if you were only trying to complete two at once.

But distractions don't just hurt work productivity. Think about what disengages you from a spouse, partner, or kids at home. What distracts you from focusing on your health? Perhaps these are some of the same factors that distract you at work. In both cases, trying to focus your attention only on the task at hand can help you finish that task—or create a meaningful memory with a child or spouse—and allow you to feel more efficient and less frazzled.

Perhaps you need to set some ground rules for yourself. The UCLA women's basketball team has a policy that when you park your car, your phone has to stay in your bag until you get to your locker. This forces everyone associated with the team to engage with teammates, staffers, and students as you enter the Mo Ostin Basketball Center. It's only a few minutes, but that's a few minutes of meaningful human interaction that might have otherwise been lost to Twitter or TikTok. The absence of your device because of a hard-and-fast rule might be the easiest way to keep it from tempting you. It's easier to say "I'm not looking at that because I'm not allowed" than it is to tell yourself "I shouldn't look at that." Discipline is easier when we can remove distractions first.

Sometimes we can't control our environments, so we employ different strategies to reduce distractions:

- Eye control, which essentially is the act of physically controlling where you look

- Music

- Disabling devices, like noise-canceling headphones

But often, it's more than a noisy office or chatty coworkers that are distracting you. Sometimes, your job might require you to be like one of those Italian judges in that study who juggled a lot of cases. Mine certainly does. If I only had one client, I would be entirely focused on that client. I like to imagine that would be one very satisfied customer. But I'd probably be broke, and you certainly wouldn't be sitting here reading my second book.

For me, balancing multiple clients requires awareness. I go back to the basics. I try to stay connected. I make sure I know what is required before I agree to something that may leave me stretched too thin.

Russell Wilson kept a checklist in his locker for the entire 2014 season. The Seahawks were coming off a Super Bowl win, and they were headed to another Super Bowl. Every day, he could look at his list and remind himself where his focus needed to stay.

1. Great balance

2. Great fundamentals

3. Be engaged

I have my own checklist for each client I work with. These are some of the items:

- **Health** Can I manage my current workload and stay healthy? (Needless to say, this has been more challenging because of the C-word.)

- **Each team** Am I serving my current clients to the best of my ability? Do I have the bandwidth to handle more work, or will taking on more negatively affect a client I'm already serving?

- **Travel** I can't be in two places at once. I have learned this the hard way.

- **Faith** Am I making sure I remain fulfilled spiritually? Am I going to church?

- **Family** Am I too wrapped up in work? How much time do I make for the important people in my life?

I also have lists that I bring along on each engagement. Top real estate agents call it a success list. Under the subtitles are boxes we created and customized that I can check off. I have them in 8" x 11" format and 5" x 7" format. When I join a team, I break down what is required of me. I may need to make notes for the coaches to emphasize to the players. I may need to make videos tailored to individual players and/or the entire team.

I also keep checklists for each player with whom I need to meet. These allow me to keep our conversations focused and on track, making those meetings more productive. When you're meeting with a Major League baseball player in a closet at some stadium before a road game, you want to make sure it's a productive conversation or you're going to lose the player's attention pretty quickly.

**Things to Do Today**
Moawad Consulting Group
**Trevor Moawad**
Today's Date _____

☐ _____
☐ _____
☐ _____
☐ _____
☐ _____
☐ _____
☐ _____
☐ _____
☐ _____

If I'm asked to speak to employees at Johnson & Johnson, I follow the same formula. I identify what the company expects its employees to get from my presentation. Once again, the operative question is this: *What does this situation require of me?* I use this information to prepare the presentation and to make sure I stay on message during my talk.

I've been using this method for a long time. It's actually what turned around my GPA in college. It helps me remind myself where my focus needs to be.

A checklist may sound like too easy a solution. But how many times have you actually stopped to create a checklist of the factors that require your focus? Do simple better. Being at your best starts with awareness and simplicity. Own the obvious.

Accept the pressure. For me, juggling work with the C-word has created tremendous pressure, but it's my current truth. So, without judgment, give each moment a life of its own. Position yourself with simple behaviors to do the basics better. Minimize distractions. Lock on to what matters; lock out everything else.

In a crisis, this becomes a must. In chapter 3, you read about Dr. Si France trying to adapt how a healthcare company designed to treat the elderly operated amid a pandemic that was killing seniors at an incredibly high rate. Si has always used checklists, but it's amazing to see how his checklists changed as the circumstances changed.

March 9, 2020, was two days before that Jazz-Thunder game in Oklahoma City got canceled. In the morning when Si wrote this checklist, America had about fifty-six hours of normal remaining.

- Stay neutral

- Be engaged

- Bring swagger

Swagger was something the CEO of a healthcare company had the luxury of thinking about on March 9. That wasn't the case on March 23. Here is Si's checklist from that day:

- Take care of your family

- Family health

- Family morale

- Take care of your parents

He also had another checklist for work:

- Stay neutral

- Focus on what you need to do

- We don't control outcomes

Those reminders kept Si focused during a critical time—not only for his business, but for his family. You've already read how the changes Si and his team made to the model gave their clients better outcomes on the whole than people in nursing homes. But Si took his first checklist as seriously as his second. During those early months of the pandemic, he and his wife tried to have "celebration dinners" as often as possible to give their three daughters something to look forward to while stuck at home. Every day, Si ran down his lists. He stayed focused on what mattered when that was absolutely critical.

But if you don't want to take it from me or from a healthcare CEO who used these techniques to get through a pandemic, take it from one of the greatest athletes who ever lived.

Serena Williams was already one of the most decorated tennis players of all time when I met her in 2010. I was working at IMG Academy in Bradenton, Florida, which started out as renowned coach Nick Bollettieri's tennis academy and then grew into a sprawling campus where elite tennis players and golfers trained alongside NFL draft prospects and the world's best young soccer or baseball players. Serena had come to Bradenton to rehab after suffering a foot infection and a pulmonary embolism. I learned a lot from her, and one of my favorite things she does is review her notes during changeovers. If you watch Serena play, watch her when the players sit down for a break before changing ends of the court. You'll see her reading from scraps of paper.

The words scribbled on the paper aren't usually earth-shattering revelations. They might be a reminder to look at the ball or to move forward during points. Serena borrowed the note-reviewing habit from older sister Venus, and Serena has been doing it for years. In fact, she was asked about it in a press conference after a match at Wimbledon in 2002. "That's just to keep me focused because sometimes I tend to lose focus when I'm out there," Serena said. "On the changeover, I tend to look around. So I just get something that I can look at to keep my focus when I'm playing."

Only once has this become an issue. In 2007, a chair umpire at the US Open told Serena she needed to put the notes away during a third-round match against Vera Zvonareva. But the ban didn't last long. The chair umpire checked with a supervisor later in the match and realized he'd been mistaken. Players weren't allowed to receive coaching notes from anyone else during a match, but they were absolutely allowed to review their own notes.

Earlier that year, Serena had deviated from her usual checklist philosophy. Before facing Maria Sharapova in the Australian Open final, Serena wrote only one word: Yetunde. Yetunde Price was Serena's half sister. She had been killed in a drive-by shooting in California in 2003. That day, Serena decided to dedicate the match to her sister's memory. So on every changeover, she stared down at Yetunde's name and locked on to the focus required to win her eighth Grand Slam title. "Every changeover I looked at it and I just thought about how happy she would have been, you know, how much she always supported me," Serena said. "I just thought about what an amazing sister she was to me. I just said, 'Serena, this has to be motivating. This has to be more than enough to motivate me.' And I think it was."

The next time you feel like you're juggling too much and you can't focus, be like Serena. Make your list. When you get a chance to take a breath, review it. If it can help the best tennis player of this century—and maybe every other one—win matches, then it can help you lock on, lock out, and stay on track.

# CHAPTER 8

# WHY YOUR PREGAME MATTERS

Four days before the biggest game Alabama had played in almost twenty years, a group of assistants hid their faces behind their game scripts so head coach Nick Saban wouldn't see them laughing as Nick quizzed me about movies. As defensive coordinator Kirby Smart, strength coach Scott Cochran, and assistant operations director Patrick Suddes struggled to keep their composure, Nick wanted to know why in the hell I wanted his team to watch an almost six-year-old hockey movie the night before they played Texas for the national title in the Rose Bowl.

To understand why this was happening in a meeting so close to such an important game, you have to understand Nick Saban. Every detail matters—including the movie the night before the game. Most coaches will take players to a theater and let them

choose from whatever is playing at that moment. Or they'll
let players vote on the movie. Not Nick. He wants every input
prior to the game to help prepare the players' minds for the
match. *Comprehensive* is probably an accurate word, but that
doesn't fully capture his level of preparation and attention to
detail across all areas of the program. I believe I lived in about
a 3 percent zone of relevance. In other words, what I did was
relevant to three hundredths of the work required to prepare for
a game like this. But every percentage point matters to Nick. So
when he shifted his attention to my corner of the operation, it
was on me to absolutely carry my weight or I'd be out. Part of
my role at the time was helping to choose the movie.

Heading into that week, I had narrowed the choices to two
movies: *Miracle* and *Invictus*. *Miracle* is the Disney-fied version
of the story of the 1980 US Olympic hockey team that won
the gold medal at Lake Placid. *Invictus* is the Clint Eastwood–
directed story of how the 1995 Rugby World Cup helped
unite post-Apartheid South Africa. *Miracle* had been released
in February 2004, and *Invictus* had hit theaters less than a
month before we traveled to California to play for the title in
early January 2010. So at this high-level meeting on game
week Wednesday—it was really a Monday, but in our minds
we had to pretend this Thursday night game was on Saturday
and count back accordingly—Nick wanted to know why I was
choosing Herb Brooks over Nelson Mandela. "Coach, I think
when you look at what message fits specifically with this team,
*Miracle* works," I said. "While *Invictus* is strong and new and in
the theaters now, I like *Miracle* for what we're facing and the
journey we've been on."

None of the players, Nick reminded me, had grown up playing hockey. Nick had read the summaries of all the new movies that Patrick had written up, so he was intrigued by the message of *Invictus*, which was about a team and a country coming together. "Anyone else have thoughts on that?" Nick asked, looking around the room. The chuckling behind the game scripts only grew louder.

"I think both points are spot on, coach," I said, buttering him up. "But when studying Clint Eastwood versus Disney, you can't compare the energy between the two films." I knew this would register with him. Pacing and runtime mattered. He wanted players engaged. He didn't want their minds wandering. Heck, Patrick had cut *Braveheart* and *Saving Private Ryan* down to two hours to meet the requirements. I'm not even sure the players knew why they were trying to save Private Ryan; I can't remember if that part made the cut. I hit Nick with the best logic I could offer. "*Miracle* is the United States versus the Soviet Union—which was a bit like us versus Florida," I said. "And beating the USSR happened in the semis like beating Florida happened in the SEC Championship. We still have to play Texas. To win the gold, they still had to beat Finland."

That's probably the first and only time in sports history that the Texas Longhorns have been compared to the Finnish national hockey team, but the analogy worked. Alabama had lost to Florida in the 2008 SEC title game, and the Gators had gone on to win the national title. Florida brought almost everyone back in 2009, and both of us were 12–0 when we played them in the SEC title game. For a lot of the country, that felt like the real national title game. In 1980, the Soviet team was a juggernaut loaded with grown men, while the US team was made up entirely of college players. Given the sport-specific circumstances and the larger backdrop of the Cold War, the semifinal game against the Soviets was so much more than a mere semifinal. And just as those American players had to put their win against the Soviets behind them—even though it was all anyone wanted to talk about—and play Finland for the gold medal, our players needed to move on from the Florida game and lock in on playing Texas. "I don't think we lose with either, coach," I said. "But I think the age of the players and the mission of Team USA and the incredible speech at the end gives us a great head space for our guys that we can follow up on."

This satisfied Nick, and he relented and moved on to much more football-specific topics. Afterward, I thanked Kirby, Scott, and Patrick for their help while I got grilled. "We knew you had it, bro," one of them said. They were still laughing.

The night before the game came, and I was just as nervous as I had been in that meeting. The Blu-Ray copy of *Miracle* we were using wouldn't work. In Nick Saban's program, running one minute late feels like running forty-five hours late. Fortunately, we had a backup copy and got the movie playing. The players, despite having no hockey backgrounds, loved it. And it gave Nick a chance to hammer home the message that we didn't win the national title when we beat Florida. There was a burnt-orange mountain to climb the next night.

After we beat Texas 37–21 to win the national title, I occasionally wondered what the Longhorns watched the night before. They adhered to the more traditional philosophy of just letting the players blow off steam and pick from what was playing. So what would they have picked that would have been in theaters in the first week of January 2010? *Avatar?* The Robert Downey Jr. *Sherlock Holmes* movie? *Alvin and the Chipmunks: The Squeakquel?*

I really hope it was that last one.

We can joke about this, but the truth is that pregame mindset matters for all of us. We may not all have scheduled competitions, but we absolutely have huge moments that we know are coming. Maybe it's a big presentation at work. Maybe it's a job interview. Maybe it's something really huge like the birth of a child. I already explained how to downshift to neutral during a stressful situation because that can help you avoid making a bad decision based on negativity or bad information. But once you can do that, you can be conscious about how you're thinking. Instead of reacting with neutral thinking, you can prepare with it. That makes it easier to downshift when stress inevitably arrives, but it also allows you to come into the moment more ready than you would have been had you simply let your mind wander wherever it wanted to go. Part of learning to live neutrally is learning to create the appropriate mindset before the big event instead of waiting for the real-world version of being down 14 in the second quarter to get yourself into neutral.

This is why I found myself watching *Cinderella Man* the night of February 2, 2020. The surgery I'd been working toward was scheduled for the next day. Months of chemotherapy had shrunken the tumors. Now Dr. Nissen would cut me open, sift around my guts, and remove what tumor was left. This didn't guarantee that I'd be done with the C-word, but so far everything had gone according to the medical team's plan. This operation would take a toll on my body. I'd have to stay in the hospital for days, and when I did get out, I'd still be very limited. I was going to hurt, and I was going to need time to heal.

I had worked with so many athletes before the biggest moments of their lives. I helped NFL hopefuls train for the combine. I helped soccer players prepare for international competitions. I helped Russell Wilson mentally prep for two Super Bowls. I helped the football players at Alabama, Florida State, and Georgia sharpen their minds before national championship games. Now I needed to use all the tools I'd developed for others to help myself enter my biggest challenge with a neutral mindset.

Two days before surgery, I talked to Michael Johnson. In 1996, Michael slipped on a pair of gold shoes and won Olympic gold in the 200 meters and the 400 meters. This made him an icon. He hadn't only dominated two of the marquee events in track; he was an American who had dominated those events at an Olympics in Atlanta. (While wearing gold spikes!) He produced metric tons of national pride, and he made himself a sports icon. But that's not why I called Michael that day.

I called Michael because he had just lived through his own medical struggle. In August 2018, Michael had just finished a workout at his home in Malibu, California, when he tripped because his ankle locked up. He sat down on a weight bench. He went back through the workout, trying to figure out if something he'd done would have caused an injury to the ankle. Then his left arm started tingling. Worried it could be something serious, Michael's wife took him to an urgent-care facility. There, the staff told Michael to go to UCLA Medical Center for more advanced testing. He got an MRI, and when it was done, his left foot was numb and he could barely move anything on his left side.

Michael was only fifty years old and he'd just had a stroke. A blood clot had forced its way through the blood vessels in his brain and left a trail of damage.

Michael being Michael, he didn't let this slow him for long. He viewed his rehab the same way he viewed training for the Olympics. He told himself he'd take the same mental approach. He would build great habits. He would celebrate incremental progress. He would consider setbacks a chance to work even harder. It helped that Michael is an elite athlete who understands his body better than most. While at first trying to move with a walker in rehab, he understood that any movement of his left foot was a victory. His natural inclination toward neutral thinking gave him a huge advantage because he understood he wasn't going to walk on day one, so he wasn't going to be heartbroken when he didn't. He just had to improve a little, like shaving a few hundredths of a second—an amount no one else would even notice—off a training time. That mindset allowed Michael to set aggressive-but-realistic goals. By the start of 2019, Michael could walk normally again. He still has occasional numbness, but he made it through the worst thanks to a champion's mentality.

There had been times during his treatment and rehab when he was frustrated or when the answers hadn't come fast enough. There had been scary times. He had dealt with versions of what I was dealing with, and it helped to get the advice of someone who had gone through their process neutrally. I told him how I had limited the flow of information to only what I needed to know. I told him how I'd tightened my circle of people around me to make sure only the people who could help me stay neutral were involved in the process.

"Do you think I'm handling this the right way?" I asked.

"Trevor, I think you're doing an incredible job," Michael said.

That gave me confidence. I knew Michael wouldn't just try to pump me up. He's not that type of person. I knew he would listen and offer advice from a place of experience. There would be no unearned optimism, only sound logic from someone who understands the process. Plus, I know Michael naturally thinks the way I have tried to train myself to think. He could guide me toward the mindset I'd need to face this operation.

Most people want a cheerleader. I never have. I can't handle people who are rah-rah when it comes to me, which I know seems odd. If you've seen me on stage talking to thousands of people from a Fortune 500 company, there's nobody more rah-rah than me. But I struggle with it as an input for my personal life.

After talking to Michael, I headed out to the hills of Palos Verdes to add some endorphins to the mix. I couldn't believe how pale I'd gotten going through chemo. Plus, the hair on my legs had fallen out. I'd never seen them like that and it freaked me out. But Michael's advice plus a good sweat helped put my mind at ease. I just needed to trust Dr. Nissen because he'd made a great plan, and this was the next step in that plan.

In this moment, I felt like one of the players I work with in my job. I had *my* mental coach—be it Michael Johnson or Lawrence Frank or Mark Herzlich, who faced the C-word while playing linebacker at Boston College and still made it to the NFL—telling me to trust the plan the coach (Dr. Nissen) made. These people did for me what I try to do for the players, and what puts them in the correct state of mind before the game starts. That way, if everything goes to hell, they have a point to which they can return. Pregaming makes downshifting easier.

At Georgia, I worked a lot with quarterback Jake Fromm. Fromm is a country boy from Warner Robins, Georgia, who loves to hunt, fish, and play football. If you saw the photos of him a few years ago in the emergency room with a lure hooked into his leg, you'd know he might love fishing a little too much. Jake originally planned to play at Alabama, but when Crimson Tide defensive coordinator Kirby Smart left Tuscaloosa in

December 2015 to become the head coach at his alma mater Georgia, Fromm began to reconsider. Kirby and offensive coordinator Jim Chaney put the hard press on Jake in the spring before his senior season in high school, and Jake decided he wanted to stay in his home state and play for the Bulldogs starting in 2017. Fromm didn't care that the Bulldogs already had Jacob Eason, the No. 1 quarterback recruit in the nation in the class of 2016. And Jake still didn't care when Eason won the starting job as a freshman. This would have scared a lot of quarterbacks away because they would assume they wouldn't get to play for at least two years, but Jake didn't care. His attitude? Bring it on.

Georgia was lucky Jake made that choice, because in the first game of the 2017 season, Jacob sprained his left knee. Jake had to take over whether he was ready or not. He had some freshman moments, but he wound up leading the Bulldogs to the SEC championship. Even after Eason came back healthy late in the season, Jake kept the job. One year removed from playing high school ball, Jake had to lead the Bulldogs against Oklahoma in the Rose Bowl. Pretty nerve-racking, right? Before that game, we—myself and Jonathan "Little Spielberg" Schultz from my staff—made Jake a video to watch the morning of the Rose Bowl on January 1, 2018, to help him find neutral.

One of Jake's favorite quarterbacks is Drew Brees, so we started the video with clips of Brees on *60 Minutes* discussing his MVP performance in the New Orleans Saints' 31–17 win against the Indianapolis Colts in Super Bowl XLIV. Brees completed 32 of 39 passes for 288 yards and two touchdowns, but he said the memories of the game tended to blur together. What he did remember was his mindset: the next play was the most important play of the game. This is the ultimate neutral statement. Everything that already happened in the game created each situation, but what happened next was up to Drew. It was a powerful message from one of Jake's idols. Next, I chose a clip of former Rams, Giants, and Cardinals quarterback Kurt Warner discussing playing in the NFL playoffs. Jake was about to play in the College Football Playoff at the most iconic venue in the sport against one of the most storied programs in the sport. I wanted Jake to understand that it was okay to acknowledge that it was special. Kirby always talks about a nameless, faceless opponent—a concept he got from Nick Saban, who got it from Bill Belichick, who got it from Bill Parcells—but sometimes, you have to prepare for the possibility that the atmosphere might be different. Maybe it's more emotional. Maybe it's more pressure packed. Maybe it's more fun. Maybe it's all of those things rolled together. That's certainly what this Rose Bowl was, so Jake needed to hear Kurt Warner say that a player can feel the tension, the excitement, and the stakes in the playoffs.

Finally, I spliced in clips of Jake performing at his best during that season. He'd played terribly when the Bulldogs visited Auburn in November. He completed less than half his throws and he got sacked four times in a 40–17 loss. But when the Bulldogs played Auburn less than a month later in the SEC Championship, he'd been great. He was efficient. He was calm. And it showed in a 28–7 win. So I wanted him to see himself

throwing a perfect deep out—one of the toughest throws in
the sport to make—to Mecole Hardman on either side of the
field. I wanted him to watch himself rip a ball down the seam
for a huge gain. I wanted him to see himself fake a toss to the
tailback, flip the ball to himself like the world's most confident
magician, and throw a touchdown pass to Isaac Nauta. This
was Jake at his best. I wanted him to see that, to remember it. If
something went wrong in the Rose Bowl, Jake could go to the
truth. He was capable of making any throw he needed to make.
He'd already done it. This, I hoped, could help him flush what
had just happened and allow him to take on the same mentality
as Drew Brees: the next play was the most important play of
the game.

After Jake watched that video, I asked him if he wanted to talk
to another guy who played a huge game in that stadium in his
first year as a college starting quarterback. I had worked with
the 2013 Florida State team that ended its season by winning a
national title against Auburn in the Rose Bowl. Jameis Winston
was a redshirt freshman on that team. He had already won the
Heisman Trophy, and no one had come close to the Seminoles
that season. I had put Jameis and Russell Wilson together so
that Russell could dispense advice, and now it was time for
Jameis—who played for the Tampa Bay Buccaneers at the
time—to pay it forward. I handed Jake the phone and stepped
out of the room to give him some privacy. As the door swung
open, I saw ESPN reporter Maria Taylor, who was working the
sideline at the game. Maria saw me and she saw that I'd been
in the room with Jake. I'm the mental coach, so people assume
players only see me when something is wrong. Maria asked

if Jake was okay. I explained that he was better than fine. He was getting valuable Rose Bowl intel from a guy who won the national title there. As I always say, you don't have to be sick to get better.

I stood on the sideline that afternoon as the sunset turned the sky purple and gold over the San Gabriel Mountains, and I was glad we'd chosen those particular messages for Jake. I had been in the Rose Bowl with Alabama and Florida State for national championship games, and the electricity in the stadium for this game matched those games. Also, this game was a damn roller coaster. The Sooners jumped out to a 31–14 lead in the second quarter, and a 55-yard Georgia field goal to end the half was the only shred of hope the Bulldogs had. But in the second half, Georgia stormed back behind tailbacks Nick Chubb and Sony Michel. When Jake threw a touchdown pass to Javon Wims to give the Bulldogs a 38–31 lead early in the fourth quarter, it felt like Georgia was completely in control.

Then it flipped again. Led by future Cleveland Brown/ insurance pitchman Baker Mayfield, the Sooners quickly tied the game. Then they took the lead less than two minutes later when Steven Parker forced a Michel fumble and then scooped it up and returned it 46 yards for a touchdown. Georgia got the ball with 3:15 remaining. If Jake couldn't get the Bulldogs down the field for a tying touchdown, the season was over. The last play had ended in utter disaster, but each next play was the game's most important. Of course Jake probably didn't need Drew Brees's advice when he faced third-and-10 on the Oklahoma 23-yard line with 1:06 remaining. Jake had to throw the ball out of bounds on the previous play because nothing had worked. Even someone who had never watched a down of football knew this was the game's most important play.

As the Oklahoma band blared, Jake got the play call from the sideline and then spoke to each of his offensive linemen, making sure they knew what to do. He and Michel consulted on where the Sooners might bring extra pressure. He clapped his hands. Center Lamont Gaillard snapped the ball. For a moment, it seemed Oklahoma linebacker Ogbonnia Okoronkwo would speed past Georgia freshman tackle Andrew Thomas, but Thomas reset his feet and pushed Okoronkwo past Jake, who sensed the pressure and slid forward while keeping his eyes downfield. Suddenly, receiver Terry Godwin broke away from an Oklahoma defender. Jake had less than a second to recognize this and throw the ball before Godwin crossed into another defender's zone. Jake fired, and suddenly third-and-10 was first-and-goal from the 7-yard line.

Georgia scored a touchdown and then went on to win the game in double overtime to advance to the national title game against Alabama. Jake, a freshman on the biggest stage in college football, hadn't melted. He had acknowledged the tension. He had acknowledged the excitement. He had faced moments where the plan fell apart and downshifted to neutral so he could focus only on the next play. His mind had been prepared in the pregame, and that preparation allowed him to perform.

I didn't have anyone to make me a video to watch before *my* big event. But just as I had for Alabama, Florida State, and Georgia,

I could choose a night-before-the-game movie to place me in the correct frame of mind. The night before my surgery, I sat with my remote in hand and scrolled through my various streaming services.

The night before my diagnosis the previous September, I had binged *Suits*. It was funny. It was mindless. It featured Meghan Markle before she became a member of the royal family. That night, I needed something light. I needed to blank out and laugh. I'd probably be learning something heavy the next day, but I wasn't going to be any sicker than I was before Dr. Nissen delivered the news. This night was different. The surgery would test me physically and mentally. My body had never been through the kind of trauma it would have to endure the following morning. I needed to feel brave. I needed something that would strengthen my spirit.

I chose *Cinderella Man*. Russell Crowe plays James Braddock, the real-life boxer who gave up the sport because of a broken hand, worked as a longshoreman, and then, in the depths of the Great Depression, returned to the sport and fought his way to the heavyweight championship of the world. I cheer every time Braddock beats Max Baer to win the title. In 2008, we had Nick show the movie to his Alabama team the night before they opened the season against Clemson in Atlanta. I hadn't seen a more locked-in group of players than the Crimson Tide in that game. They were underdogs according to Las Vegas, but they destroyed Clemson and set the tone for the next decade-plus of Alabama football. One sleep away from a surgery that could change my life, I wanted to feel the way those players had felt one sleep away from the game that announced to the nation that Alabama was back among the nation's elite.

The next morning, I went to the American Martyrs Church in Manhattan Beach. I chatted with the big man for a few minutes. Then I went for a walk with my ex-wife, Solange, whose love is as pure as it gets. As we walked downhill toward the Pacific Ocean, I kept repeating the same phrase: take the next step. This was my version of Drew Brees saying the next play is the most important play.

When I arrived at the hospital, I donned the gown that would be my uniform for the next few days. I also slid on some yellow grippy socks that I'd be staring down at once I came out of surgery. Russell Crowe as James Braddock had lifted my spirits. Talking to God had filled my heart. Walking with Solange had reminded me that I had a team standing behind me. Now I just had to do it. I turned my phone on myself and began shooting a video.

"Up until this point, I've been really nervous and scared," I said. "I'm not scared anymore. Now I'm like game day. I've got my mind right. I've got it right where it needs to go. I'm just excited to be in a great state physically for this doctor so I can do everything I can to get this thing out and move on to the next step—living life."

But, just as the games don't always go the way we visualized, it's never that easy.

When it came time to put me under, the nurses insisted that I roll over on my stomach. This may have been part of their plan, but no one had told me that. In all of my previous procedures during my treatment, I'd been on my back when I received anesthesia. For my comfort, being on my back was pivotal. It made me feel safer. But they kept going, making preparations to put me on my stomach and then put me out. Finally, I spoke up. "Can I please be on my back?" I asked. That wasn't protocol, I was told. If I went under while on my back, they'd have to flip me. As I tried to discuss the issue further, the conversation began to feel like an argument. I needed to get back to neutral and, for my sake, I needed everyone else in neutral as well. I told everyone I needed two minutes to get my mind in a better place. And I said I needed everyone else in a good place as well. As it turned out, the anesthesiologist had no problem administering while I was on my back. So everyone—especially me—cooled down. All that pregame preparation had allowed me to snap back to neutral. Now I was ready.

I started progressive muscle relaxation. I controlled my breathing. Breathe in for four counts. Hold for four counts. Release for four counts. I thought of the room I stayed in as a child at my grandparents' house in Kalama, Washington. I could smell the marshmallow cookies my grandmother made. (I can still smell them today.) I put two thumbs up, and I went down.

When I awoke, Solange was next to my bed. So was Russell Wilson. I had taken the next step. And I was ready for that step because of my pregame preparation.

As you just read, you don't have to be Russell prepping for a playoff game to go through a pregame process. Maybe you have to make a presentation in front of a bunch of coworkers but you're terrified of speaking in public. This is also a situation that requires optimum performance, so it should be handled just like an athlete would handle game preparation. That includes practice, but it also should include mental preparation so that when it's time to perform, your mind is precisely where it needs to be.

If you're giving that presentation, of course you're going to run through what you're going to say. Of course you're going to make sure your laptop works with the projector. (Or now that remote work is all the rage, you'll make sure you know exactly how to share your screen on Zoom.) This is the equivalent of Russell going to practice and throwing to Tyler Lockett and D. K. Metcalf. But you also need to go through the kind of mental preparation that Russell goes through with me before each game.

I can't make you a video that will show you all the times you've talked to these coworkers before, but comb through your personal memory bank. You know these people. You've worked with them for years. You've gone to happy hour with them. You've told them stories, and they've told you stories. That relationship doesn't change just because you've got to show them some graphs and explain how the company can maximize revenue. This is the equivalent of showing Jake Fromm examples of himself throwing a perfect deep out. If he feels any trepidation on game day, he can dial up that scene in his mind and know he's capable. You can do the same when it comes time to give your presentation. You're not facing a judge and defending your life. This is just Ted from business development who forgot to bring diapers the first time he took his baby daughter to the grocery store. It's just Beth from accounting whose favorite drink is called an Alabama Slammer. You don't need to be intimidated by these people. You've prepared for this.

The night before your presentation, try a pregame movie. Maybe you pick *Office Space* just to remind you how absurd all of this really is. Maybe that helps relieve the pressure. Or maybe you want to get pumped so you can inspire those coworkers. *Any Given Sunday* has an all-time, hair-on-your-arms-standing-up speech from Al Pacino about fighting for that inch a football team may need to gain to win a game. That one will leave you ready to push your colleagues to greater heights. Perhaps you want to get really literal about your fear of public speaking. Go with *The King's Speech* and watch Colin Firth as newly crowned King George VI overcome a stutter so he can speak to a much larger audience than you will. The secret is to decide how you want to feel when it's time to perform and choose something that will put you in that frame of mind.

On the day of your presentation, review the steps you've taken to prepare again. These are the facts you can fall back on to get yourself back to neutral if your mind starts to spin out of control. Go through your mental file of similar situations where you've succeeded—or at least survived. This will settle you as the moment approaches. Just before, think back to your pregame movie. If you chose *Office Space*, think about Peter dismantling the cubicles or beating the printer with a baseball bat. Laugh. Remember that this doesn't have to be so serious. If you chose *Any Given Sunday*, think about the way Pacino started his inch-by-inch speech calmly and then built to a crescendo that had everyone ready to run through a wall. If you chose *The King's Speech*, remember when the new king yells "I have a voice," and remember that you have one too.

Hopefully, you didn't choose the *Squeakquel*. That never worked for anyone.

In all seriousness, choose what fits. What matters is that you prepare with a purpose. And don't forget that your mind and your body are connected. If you're a person who needs to get your blood flowing to face the day, make sure you get a workout in the morning of your presentation. If you get sleepy or queasy on a full stomach, make sure you go in with an empty one. If you require some sustenance to perform your best, then maybe you need to pregame like I did when I was going through chemotherapy.

My chemo sessions were long days. I was prescribed three drugs—Gemzar, Abraxene, and Cisplatin—and, on the day of my first session, I entered the facility in the morning and didn't leave until after Russell's Monday Night Football game against the 49ers was over. (I was on the West Coast, so it wasn't midnight, but I'd still spent most of a day there.) Part of my pregame plan that first day was to tell the staff that I didn't want to hear anything about potential side effects. I told them to give me a pamphlet. What I didn't tell them was

I never intended to read it. If the side effects hit me, then they hit me. But I wasn't going to fill my head with a bunch of scary possibilities that might never happen. How would that help? (And I have no idea if this had anything to do with the outcome, but my side effects from chemo were minimal.) My other pregame strategy for those chemo sessions came from a guy who had been through the C-word himself.

In 2009, Mark Herzlich was a twenty-one-year-old stud linebacker at Boston College. He'd been named the Atlantic Coast Conference (ACC) defensive player of the year in 2008, and he had a bright football future ahead of him. But as he worked out to prepare for his senior season, he couldn't shake the pain in his left leg. It was in his thigh and sometimes it would radiate back around to his hamstring. A doctor worried Mark had suffered nerve damage, so he ordered an MRI. That doctor called with the results and told Mark he needed to consult another specialist: an oncologist. After more tests, Mark learned he had Ewing's sarcoma, a form of the C-word that affects the bones. Mark then learned that if doctors couldn't confirm that the disease was isolated, they'd have to amputate his lower leg. Fortunately, it remained isolated. So Mark started an aggressive chemotherapy regimen. And it worked. Mark returned to Boston College for the 2010 season, and then he played seven seasons for the New York Giants. He even helped win a Super Bowl. Through seven months of chemotherapy, Mark learned a lot. But the most important might have been this: eat.

"Food is a premium, and they will tell you that you'll lose weight. But you don't have to," Mark told me. "I ate anything

I could to sustain weight, and though my treadmill workouts and lifts were far from where they were, I maintained as much of my normal schedule as I could. Like you say, Trev. Control everything you can, and there are things you can control."

So I decided to fuel with French toast. That was mission critical on those early mornings when I got ready for chemo with Jon Schultz, my first mate from Moawad Consulting. We'd walk a few blocks to the northern end of Manhattan Beach and post up in a breakfast surf shop. I powered down as much French toast as I could. I normally eat pretty healthily, but I wanted calories in bulk to power me through this challenge, so I got two orders of French toast with sides of sourdough bread. Some of you who have sworn off carbs may have fainted when you read that, but when you're trying to manage chemotherapy, you take the advice of the people who handled it well. In my mind, the more bread I could take in, the more my body would absorb the mixture of chemicals coming in without spiraling off into side effects. I have no idea if that's what actually happened. All I know is I wasn't scared when they dripped those drugs into my body, and I didn't have the side effects that sound so scary when they write about them in the pamphlets that I definitely didn't read.

If you do everything you can to prepare your mind, you can stay neutral no matter what.

# CHAPTER 9

# YOU ARE YOUR OWN GENERAL MANAGER

My dad traveled a lot, but he always left me little reminders so he could stay relevant to my life in Seattle from wherever he was. Before he left for every trip, he'd stick multicolored Post-it notes on my bathroom mirror. Some of the notes contained messages of affection. Some reminded me of behaviors I needed to continue in order to reach my goals. Some contained quotes about whatever I was doing at the time, be it basketball, soccer, theater, or a math test. One of those quotes has always stuck with me: "It takes each of us to make the difference for all of us."

In a team environment—whether it's a sports team, a company, or a family—we all have weight to carry. Everyone matters. Collective consciousness is a real thing. It allows us to help one another drive forward to a common goal. The right team is a major competitive advantage. We know that in sports. When you add Kevin Durant to a Golden State Warriors team that already has Steph Curry, Klay Thompson, and Draymond Green, you get an even more amazing team. When you're the Tampa Bay Buccaneers and you add Tom Brady and Rob Gronkowski and win a Super Bowl, you make sure you re-sign the other key pieces to that team like Lavonte David and Shaquill Barrett and Chris Godwin. We know that in business. When a job at your company opens, do you want your CEO to hire a buddy, or do you want your CEO to hire someone who has already performed the job at a high level? Of course you want the experienced expert. We don't even have to think about these answers because they're so obvious.

In sports, general managers and team presidents become rock stars when they can assemble the best rosters. Coaches tinker with lineups to produce the best chemistry. And we celebrate when that chemistry works. Of course LeBron James wants to play with Anthony Davis. But LeBron also loves playing with Alex Caruso, who isn't nearly as good as Anthony Davis but who plays a complementary role that makes the Lakers much better. As the Lakers worked toward the NBA title in 2020, *The Wall Street Journal*[1] declared balding former G-Leaguer Caruso "The LeBron of playing with LeBron." At the time, the Lakers' net rating—a measure of how much better or worse a team is when a specific player or set of players is on the court—when LeBron and Davis were on the floor at the same time was plus-8. That's really good. The net rating when LeBron and Caruso were on the floor together? Plus-18.6. That's astounding. It turns out Caruso is a natural at playing with

LeBron. He knows how to set a screen and get the hell out of the way so LeBron can work. He knows how to operate in space to give LeBron the options he likes the best. James told the *Journal* that playing with Caruso "gives our team a sense of calmness."

Do you have an Alex Caruso in your life? Would you even know how to measure whether you did?

For more than twenty years, I've kept my eyes open. I've watched the Alabama and Florida State teams that won. I've watched the Michigan football teams that lost. I've watched the US men's national soccer teams that were up and down. I've watched "individual" sport stars like Maria Sharapova (tennis), Paula Creamer (golf), or Jeff Gordon (auto racing) as they built the teams around them to help them succeed. Some of those teams hosted their off-site meetings right outside my office in Bradenton, and many times they allowed me to sit in. I paid attention.

What I learned is that we don't think nearly enough about how we should be acting as the general manager or team president in our own lives. What teammates are we choosing to help us navigate the challenges life throws at us? Do we have a lead-off hitter who gives us a spark? Do we have an offensive tackle who can protect us? Do we have a rebounding power forward who can help us bounce back when we miss?

As the C-word became a real part of my life, I recognized I needed to evaluate my team. Not the employees of my company, but the people in my life. I needed to determine what roles each person could play. I also needed to accept that there might be some people who didn't need to know about my diagnosis or my treatment because it wouldn't help either of us if they did. At forty-five, this was entirely my call. I had no real experience doing this, but I'd watched how winners were built in the world of sports, military units, and in Fortune 500 companies. I recognize the powerful impact the right team can make on the individual.

The process of building a winning team isn't that different at Alabama or Naval Special Warfare or Johnson & Johnson or in a personal battle with the C-word. Working with the organizations I've worked with was a blessing, and those experiences cemented critical truths in my mind. It's less about building a winning "soccer" team or "medical" team than it is about building a winning team in general. There are differences relative to the mission, of course, but far more similarities than we realize. This equipped me for my own journey. I'd seen so many winning teams. Not in theory, but on the field or on the base or in the boardroom. I'd seen so much transference and used so many of the same concepts between teams—athletic and otherwise. These concepts were universal.

As I navigated the world of the C-word, I resolved to be very deliberate in building my team. I couldn't just go on a free-agent signing spree. I also couldn't put everyone on my existing roster in the game. I needed people who could help me deal with fear and pain and sudden changes. I didn't need to involve people who couldn't handle the information or who had their own major struggles to conquer. Part of this decision came from working with teams. I had seen how much the addition of a key role player could help, and I also had seen how one high-maintenance player could siphon off the energy of everyone else in the locker room. I couldn't afford to have any energy siphoned off. Another factor in this decision stemmed from—like so many other things in my life—my dad.

I'll never forget the winter of 1999. It was my fourth and final year as a high school teacher. I lived in Delray Beach, Florida, with my then-girlfriend, Danielle. Danielle and I had been in Seattle for the holidays a month earlier. That's when I first noticed the slightest of differences in my father.

He asked me to go to Mercer Island High School and present to their basketball team with him over the Christmas break. I'd watched him speak to groups for years, but I had never participated. I was prepared, though. I had taken electives in sports psychology in college. Besides teaching and coaching at the high school level, I was working part time on the mental preparation side for John and Chris Evert at their tennis academy in Boca Raton. I'd been taking my dad's educational content and starting to modify it in key areas so that it made more sense in the sports world, so I definitely had something to offer. And I had the utmost respect for the guy who had invited us. Coach Ed Pepple ran the Mercer Island basketball program, and he was a legend in the state of Washington. He had coached Steve Hawes, who starred at Washington and then spent ten years in the NBA. He also coached Quin Snyder, who went on to play at Duke before moving into coaching. Quin was the head coach at Missouri before moving into the NBA, where he served as an assistant for four years before becoming the head coach of the Utah Jazz in 2014. Coach Pepple was a tremendous molder of people, and he was great at helping his players understand the team dynamic. His players didn't say "I." They said "we."

In a surprise move on that day, my dad had me do about 75 percent of the presentation to about forty players and coaches. We had a blast. As we said our goodbyes to their staff, we walked into the parking lot and he asked me to drive home. This struck me as very strange. In my twenty-three years of living—and seven years of driving—he'd never asked me to drive home. It gnawed at me. When I got the call a month later, I connected the dots.

I was back in Florida, and on the other end of the line my dad shared the news of this illness he'd been diagnosed with. He had the C-word. Being Bob Moawad, he immediately outlined the tentative plan he'd put in place. I don't remember specifics. I remember sadness. I held Danielle's hand and just listened without attempting to create counter-narratives.

Afterward, I walked outside along the bike path and just let myself feel everything. The memory that sticks, as tough as it is to admit, was how disappointing this all was to my mom. My dad had planned to live forever. He thought he would teach until he was ninety-five. He was a superhero. He and my mom had purchased their second home in Arizona just years earlier and were finally positioned to spend more time together. That plan had been destroyed by the disease.

I was across the country, not in the trenches, but I knew my dad
would let me know how best I could support him as he built out
his own team. I later found out that the role my dad wanted me
to play in his life was to live mine—period. He wanted to hear
my voice on the phone reporting on the evolution of my career
as I moved from education into the sports world. I sensed the
resentment in my mother. She had believed my dad would live
forever and struggled for years to reconcile the expectation with
the reality and the consequent weight she was forced to carry.
Just before their empty nest life was supposed to really begin, the
C-word took over. My dad fought until January 2007. My mom
did an amazing job on the outside, but inside, understandably,
she struggled to handle that burden with grace.

Simply put, I didn't want to put that burden on anyone else
if I could possibly avoid it. I didn't want to create resentment.
These challenges can dramatically affect the people in our
worlds. They can force our friends and loved ones into horrible
positions. I wasn't going to do that.

I appeared on the *Better Together* podcast with former *E! News*
anchor Maria Menounos in January 2020,[2] just days before my
first major surgery. I had already been through chemotherapy—
though a lot of people in my life didn't know that yet—and
Maria was talking about helping her mother fight the C-word.
(Unfortunately, Litsa Menounos passed away in May 2021
at age sixty-six.) Our conversation turned to which people
you can talk to or solicit advice from in those situations.
Without revealing that I was dealing with that very issue in
my own life, I offered some advice of my own. "You need to

understand people in your life who are not good with that type of information," I said. "You need to not put them in a position to disappoint you." Then Maria made a great point. "You don't need someone to come bring you cookies and say 'I'm so sorry. You poor thing,'" she said. I certainly didn't need that. But Maria and I agreed that you have to accept that you're going to hurt some feelings by excluding certain people from your circle of trust. But in a critical situation such as the one I was dealing with, or the one Maria's mom was dealing with, other people's feelings can't be your priority. "You have to protect you," I said, "or you have to protect your mom."

The C-word is different for everyone. This was my experience. I had decided that, knowing the way I'm built, the best way to get through it was inside out, not outside in. No amount of people yelling "RAH, RAH, YOU CAN DO IT" would make me feel any better. The fewer people involved, the better.

At least that's what I thought at first. I had resolved to keep the circle extraordinarily tight because I didn't want to put that burden on anyone else if I could avoid it. But one of the people I did want in the circle convinced me I needed to broaden it a bit. And I listened because he had already lived through what I was going through.

I met Mark Herzlich in 2011 as he trained to jump from Boston College to the NFL. By the time I met him, Herzlich already had a reputation as one of the toughest football players on the planet. Not for his ability to shed blocks and stuff running backs—though he'd been very good at that as a college linebacker—but because he'd beaten the C-word and returned to the field.

I told you a little about Mark in the pregame chapter. He was a first-team All-American and the ACC Defensive Player of the Year in 2008. As he prepared for his senior season in 2009, pain in his upper left leg intensified. He suspected nerve damage, but an MRI revealed something suspicious, so Mark went to an oncologist. The diagnosis was Ewing's sarcoma, a rare form of the C-word that affects the bones.

Mark had two options after chemotherapy. He could try to target the area with radiation, or he could let doctors cut out a piece of his femur and replace it with a prosthetic or a piece from a cadaver. If he had the surgery, he'd never play football again, and there was no guarantee he'd be able to walk normally again. If radiation worked, Mark would have a much better chance of normal mobility for the rest of his life and might have a chance to play football again. Doctors might be able to insert a metal rod in his femur that would make it as strong as it was before. But there was a massive risk. While getting a second opinion about a potential procedure to insert the rod, Mark learned that if the radiation didn't work, then he probably couldn't fall back on the surgical option. The radiation could make his bone so brittle that it couldn't handle a prosthetic or a piece from a cadaver. They'd probably have to amputate the leg.

Doctors gave Mark a week to weigh his options and make a decision. The surgical option gave him the best chance at long-term survival, but it would mean the end of football and might mean a life of compromised mobility. The radiation option might give him a chance to play football again, but if it didn't work, the result could be catastrophic. As he tried to decide, Mark sought the advice of his father, Sandy. "Dad, what would you do?" Mark asked. "I know what I'd do if I were you," Sandy replied. "And I know what I would tell you to do as your parent. Those are two different things." Mark grasped what his dad meant then, but he didn't truly understand until he had his own children. Now in his thirties with two kids, Mark isn't so sure he would have made the same choice. He probably needed to be a twenty-one-year-old who didn't have the same fear of mortality as an older person.

He chose the radiation and, with each successive scan, the prognosis got more optimistic. The bad cells were destroyed, and, even better, the radiation didn't make his bone too brittle to reinforce. When doctors had determined the treatments had done their job, they cleared Mark to have the metal rod inserted in his femur. If he was up to it, he could try to return to football.

Mark had missed the entire 2009 season, but he had time to train for 2010. While training, he broke his hand and sustained a stress fracture in his foot. It didn't stop him from playing. He played limited snaps in the season opener against Weber State, and even though he had his injured foot wrapped so tight he could barely feel his toes, he felt no pain on the field. He wasn't scared of getting hit in the thigh that had received so many radiation treatments. He made two observations that day: he'd never take football for granted again, and he really needed to knock off the rust.

Playing alongside future NFL superstar Luke Kuechly, Mark had a good senior season. But he wasn't the wrecking machine he'd been before the C-word. NFL general managers, who tend to be risk-averse regarding medical issues they're not intimately familiar with, steered clear of Mark in the draft. They didn't want to take a chance on a guy who had beaten a disease none of them had ever heard of. After going undrafted, Mark signed with the New York Giants. He had no idea if he'd make the team, but on the day of final cuts in 2011, he sat in his hotel room hoping his phone wouldn't ring before the 4 p.m. deadline to trim the roster to fifty-three.

It rang.

It was Mark's dad, asking if Mark wanted he and Mark's mom to drive up from Philadelphia to offer in-person support. No, Mark said. He wanted to wait by himself.

The deadline came and went, and no news meant good news. The phone rang again. It was Sandy again.

"You sure you don't want us to come up?"

Mark relented. "Sure, come up."

"Good," Sandy said. "We're in the lobby."

They'd been waiting there all day. After all they'd been through, they'd earned the celebratory dinner that night.

But Mark didn't only make the Giants. He was a special teams ace who earned playing time at linebacker as well. And his rookie season ended in the most amazing way possible. The Giants rebounded from a four-game losing streak to win three of their last four and make the playoffs. Then they beat the Falcons, the Packers, and the 49ers to win the NFC title. As Mark got off the plane in Indianapolis to prepare for Super Bowl XLVI against the Patriots, he thought back to all that had happened in less than three years. He had gone from *if you choose incorrectly, you could lose your leg and maybe still die* to playing in the Super Bowl. My life, Mark thought, is a fairy tale. And when the Giants won that game 21–17, Mark got the fairy tale ending.

Mark played with the Giants until 2018. Since his retirement, he's been working for ESPN's ACC Network. He's also fielded quite a few phone calls from me. Because he'd lived through this, I knew he'd understand what I was dealing with in ways that other people probably wouldn't. Early in the process, it was clear he understood what I was dealing with much better than even I did.

While his tip to load up on carbs before chemo treatments was clutch, he also gave me some more macro advice. For instance, it's okay to be angry. It's okay to be scared. My whole life has been about avoiding the negative, but when you get diagnosed with the C-word, those emotions are completely unavoidable.

They're a natural human response to that kind of news, and it's unnatural to suppress them. Mark reminded me to let that energy out of my body. That helped get me back to neutral.

The most important piece of advice Mark gave me was to stop trying to do it alone. I had explained to him all the reasons why I wanted so few people to know what I was dealing with, and he understood. Even though far more people knew about his situation when he got sick because Boston College had to explain why the reigning ACC defensive player of the year wasn't playing, Mark still tried to minimize the burden he put on others. Early on, he wouldn't even tell his parents how sick he felt. He wanted to be their rock even though it should have been the other way around. Mark realized quickly he couldn't keep doing that. "It was way too much for me to handle alone," Mark said, so he started letting more people into his battle and it made a world of difference. Instead of shouldering an additional burden, he had people fighting with him.

Mark understood why I had taken my approach because he had already taken it. He knew that I had done it in part to maintain the tiniest semblance of control as this thing in my body turned my life upside down. But that control costs too much mental and physical energy to maintain when you need that energy to fight. So I had to let go of some control, but what I got in return was a team capable of helping me.

Another great piece of advice Mark gave me was to pray. Mark was relatively early in his education as a Christian when he got diagnosed, but he had been reading in the Bible and listening to sermons about people asking God to help them carry the weight in their lives. So he tried it. As Mark prayed, he said, "They said, 'Cast your burdens on me. Cast your anxieties on me, so I'm doing that, and I need you right now." That brought Mark peace.

I took Mark's advice. As many times as I could, I went to church and prayed. When the pandemic caused churches to close their doors, I parked in the church parking lot and prayed. I also realized I couldn't do this alone. I needed God. And Mark was right. As much as I didn't want to burden anyone, I needed other people. Mark was a key part of my dream team but, thanks to him, I added a few more spots to the roster.

In the fall of 2019, I was living on The Strand in Manhattan Beach. I had moved there from suburban Phoenix essentially to restart my life after my divorce. I figured living in a place with so much energy—and one hell of a view—would jumpstart my reentry into single life as well as give me a great place to unwind when I wasn't on the road with Georgia's football team or the New York Mets. I could step out my door on Marine Street and be on the coast of the Pacific Ocean in one of the most epic surf areas known to man. But instead of taking dates down the picturesque beachside sidewalk, I usually wound up walking or jogging alongside an NBA executive.

Lawrence Frank is the president of basketball operations for the Los Angeles Clippers. In 2020, he was named the NBA's executive of the year. He and I met through Billy Schmidt, who at the time was working on Billy Donovan's staff with the Oklahoma City Thunder. Billy Schmidt is a huge college football fan, so he knew of me from my work at Alabama and Florida State. He helped get me hooked up with the Thunder for a few years, but part of my plan for my new life was to try to find more work within my own community. I didn't need to spend as much time on airplanes and in hotels. So I met with Lawrence with the hope of working for a team based a few miles from my house. Lawrence and I hit it off, and he introduced me to Doc Rivers, who was coaching the Clippers at the time. I got Doc's stamp of approval, and then I met the other members of the front office. They liked what I taught because it wasn't, as Lawrence puts it, "Pollyanna stuff." Pro athletes have finely tuned bullshit detectors, and they have no time for people who think they can solve every problem in a single session. They would much rather deal with someone who knows they're going to have to work very hard to get what they want. Lawrence and the other Clippers executives respected that I didn't sugarcoat anything or suggest that there is some magic pill. Because there isn't.

Lawrence and the Clippers hired me to be a strategic advisor focusing on mental performance. We quickly became friends, but it wasn't until after I woke up with yellow eyes that I understood how great a friend Lawrence truly was. He was the anchor of my team.

It helped that Lawrence understood prolonged health battles after helping his wife deal with chronic medical issues. He had seen firsthand the frustration of treatment delays and slow communication between doctors and seemingly endless strings of appointments. He understood my day-to-day experience first as doctors tried to diagnose me and then as they tried to treat me.

During those walks—or, when I was feeling better, runs— along the beach, he listened. He understood what I teach because I had worked with his team, so Lawrence could offer advice in language that really connected with me. I may be the guy teaching this stuff to others, but I'm still human. Sometimes I need help getting back to neutral also. Lawrence was always willing to provide a nudge away from negative back to where I needed to be. He knew this would be a long, drawn-out process, and he reminded me to stay in the moment when my mind started to drift toward the big picture. When dealing with the C-word, you'll be miserable if you try to scoreboard-watch. Outcomes are unpredictable and subject to change, so worrying about them will only overwhelm. If Lawrence sensed that I was getting overwhelmed, he was able to help me navigate back to neutral. If I had a setback, Lawrence reminded me that what just happened doesn't predict the next moment.

Lawrence also helped in a key area: talent acquisition. I needed to get the very best people to oversee my process. Lawrence's literal job is building rosters. He was my No. 1 draft choice for my team, and he immediately began helping me in ways that continue to amaze me. He pointed me toward Clippers' team doctor Steve Krems because he knew Dr. Krems would be a great point guard from a medical standpoint. In all those years running onto the field with the Crimson Tide or the Seminoles or the Bulldogs, I knew how important it was to your own confidence to be surrounded by the "Top Guns" in any given field. Dr. Krems helped put the medical version of my team together.

It was up to me to select the other key members of the support team that eventually helped me through the scariest time of my life. I chose people I knew could handle it. More importantly, they chose to help me. They lent their time, their attention, their wisdom, and an awful lot of emotional energy. And for that, I'm forever grateful.

You've met Mel Tucker, the Michigan State football coach who used neutral thinking to guide his team through a year where the challenges never stopped coming. But when I got diagnosed, Mel was starting his first season at Colorado. He and I had grown close when he worked as an assistant at Alabama and later at Georgia, and he truly understood what I teach. Like me, Mel is not a rah-rah person. He wants the truth and that's all.

Mel is exactly the kind of person I needed. We talked on the phone frequently, and he visited me as I recovered from my first surgery. He's a natural motivator; he's great at getting players to tap into their inner fire. He did the same with me. But there were also times when he just listened. Those who know me well might say I tend to ramble, but those same people would tell you that sometimes those verbal detours lead to breakthroughs for me. There were times during chemotherapy or during recovery from surgery that I just needed to talk out my feelings, and Mel provided a sounding

board. Because he understands how my mind works, he was
able to steer me toward neutral. He never, ever bullshit me,
and that was critical at a time when false positivity could have
created unreasonable expectations.

Also, Mel believed in me. He didn't have to say it. He showed
it. Even though I was recovering from one major surgery and
headed toward another one, and even though the pandemic
had made it impossible for outside consultants such as myself
to do in-person work with college football teams, Mel
still hired me to help his staff and his team as he made the
transition to Michigan State. It was a vote of confidence that
he expected me to help the Spartans for a while, and, even
though I'm not letting myself look too far down the road, it
was reassuring to know somebody still had plans for me in
the future.

You know Russell Wilson, whose day job is playing
quarterback for the Seattle Seahawks. He's about as busy
as it gets, but he always made time for me. Also, his faith
helped give me faith.

DJ Eidson is one of my partners in the company Limitless
Minds, and, like Russell, his faith is powerful. DJ could always
lift me up.

You've also met Jon Schultz, the Moawad Consulting Group's
director of multi-media services. I call him "Little Spielberg,"
because he creates videos that bring my ideas to life and helps

reinforce those ideas for the players we work with. He's also a loyal friend. He went far above and beyond his job description, and I'll always be grateful for that. He was with me at nearly every chemo treatment. He helped me move while I recovered from surgery. He was there any time I needed him. He's a young, married guy, and he didn't need to be wasting his time with me. But I'm glad he did.

Chris Brearton is the chief operating officer of MGM Studios. For a time, he was my roommate in Manhattan Beach. He made life feel normal even when it absolutely wasn't.

Jeff Allen is Alabama's associate athletic director for sports medicine. He's one of the most trusted athletic trainers in America, and with good reason. Players know immediately that Jeff cares about them. He helps them recover from their injuries any way he can. He also lends an ear when they're scared.

Jeff and I arrived at Alabama on the same day in 2007, and we bonded immediately. Because I'd known him so long, I wasn't afraid to be emotional with him. I could pray with him. I could cry on the phone and not feel the least bit self-conscious about it. There isn't a voice I'd rather hear when I'm about to be wheeled into surgery.

Michael Johnson owns four Olympic gold medals, one very famous pair of gold track spikes, and the patience of a saint. He listened as I went over my treatment plan, and his calmness calmed me. I first met Michael years ago when he came to IMG Academy to impart wisdom on some youngsters preparing for the NFL draft. One of those guys was Drew Brees, who retired after the 2020 season, so none of us is that young anymore. Listening to Michael back then helped me understand the value of a plan when chasing a dream. He still understands the value of a great plan, and after watching him attack rehab after his stroke, I wanted his approval on any treatment or rehab plans for me.

Solange Moawad didn't have to do anything for me. Our divorce was finalized in 2019. Any obligation she had no longer existed. Yet she was with me before every procedure. We had both worked hard after the divorce to keep a strong relationship, but she went above and beyond.

Ingrid Walters wasn't someone I knew before this, but hers was a friendly face I kept seeing during my treatment. Sometimes, it's comforting to know you aren't the only one in the world going through what you're going through.

These people supported me when I needed them most. They helped give me strength when I had none. They listened when I needed to talk. They understood when I needed to cry.

Even if you aren't going through a crisis in your life, you need to keep a running tally of the people you could lean on in a catastrophe. If you don't feel like your circle of friends and family contains enough of those people, widen your circle. In the best of times, a team can make life more fun. In the worst of times, a team can keep you afloat.

These are the types of people you need to find and keep in your life . . .

- Find people who aren't worried about what your situation is doing to them. Every single person I mentioned above asked, "How can I help?" instead of "How does this affect me?"

- Find people who can connect you with others who can help. My first big win was Lawrence connecting me with Dr. Krems, who then connected me with the correct specialists.

- Find people who speak your language. Having Mel and Lawrence, who understand the neutral mindset so well, made communicating concerns easier. They also knew how to pull me back from the edge and push me back toward neutral. Russell helped me build the vocabulary, so he knew exactly what to say.

- Find people you aspire to be like. I wish my mind worked like Michael Johnson's. I wish I could be as tough as Mark Herzlich.

- Find people who share your faith. Mark reminded me that even though I had a bunch of rock star doctors on my side, prayer also could make me feel better. Praying with Jeff helped give me strength when I needed it most. Talking to DJ and Russell strengthened my resolve every time.

- Find people who love you no matter what. Solange didn't have to be there. She had my back anyway.

- Don't be afraid to add a free agent to help your championship push. I didn't know Ingrid before this, but sharing our experience helped make us both stronger.

So don't wait. Start evaluating your roster today. You don't have to be like an NFL general manager on cutdown day and start slashing. But you do need to honestly assess everyone in your life and then start building your depth chart. What do the people in your life bring to the table? Do you have a complete team now, or do you need to add some different skill sets to the roster?

That way, when adversity strikes, you already have your support system in place. You won't even think about trying to do it alone.

# CHAPTER 10

# EVERYONE NEEDS A COACH

I got a call in 2016 that blew my mind. It was from a member of Maria Shriver's staff. I was living in Arizona at the time, and Maria was planning to be in the area and wanted to meet.

I got confused and called tennis player Maria Sharapova's agent to confirm details because Maria Sharapova's people calling me would have made sense. I had worked with a ton of tennis players, and I knew Maria from my time at IMG Academy.

But this wasn't Maria Sharapova who wanted to meet. It was Maria Shriver. NBC News Maria Shriver. Emmy and Peabody Award winner Maria Shriver. CEO Maria Shriver. Philanthropist Maria Shriver. Former first lady of California Maria Shriver. John F. Kennedy's niece Maria Shriver. What could she possibly need from me?

It turned out she wanted to give me a great idea. She'd read about my work with Russell Wilson, and she wanted to know if I'd ever thought of expanding my coaching beyond athletes. She explained that a lot of the tools I was sharing with athletes were applicable in the business world. She said they could be especially useful to many women who might be reentering the workforce after having children. She also said those lessons could help the people who manage other people. This group, by the way, includes parents trying to turn their kids into good, productive people.

And she was right. I've taken her advice and expanded my scope beyond sports, and there are so many parallels. The same neutral thinking techniques that work for Russell Wilson or Pete Alonso absolutely can help a person coming back into the working world after taking a few years off. They can help keep that person from getting overwhelmed by change. They can help that person juggle work life and home life. They can help that person compete for promotions.

But the point Maria made that truly stuck with me is that everyone needs a coach. We all have to lead at some point in our lives, whether we're someone's boss at work or whether we're a parent responsible for the upbringing of small humans. And the best way to lead is to lead like a coach. This is how Maria put it, and it's perfect. "Find what people do well, and then encourage them to do more. That's the great thing about a coach, right? It's knowing what the person does well, and then helping them visualize what you see in them that they can do better."

I was raised by a coach in more ways than one. My dad started out as a basketball coach, but then he evolved into a mental coach as he carved out a career in a field that barely existed when he started working in it. But no matter how big he got, no matter how many people were in the audience, he never stopped addressing people the way he addressed his team because my dad understood what a coach's job is—no matter the venue. A coach is someone who accepts the responsibility to develop, challenge, and support people (individually or collectively) who have asked for guidance. If this also sounds to you like the definition of a good teacher or an excellent parent, you're not wrong.

The first world-class coach I met was Nick Bollettieri. In 2001, I was fairly new at IMG Academy. My then-boss Chad Bohling invited me into his office to watch Nick explain to a reporter from HBO's *Real Sports* why a thirteen-year-old Russian tennis player was going to be a superstar. That player? Sharapova.

As I listened to Nick lay out what he saw as Maria's path to greatness, I understood why he had been so successful. Of course Nick had recognized Sharapova's work ethic, competitiveness, and discipline, and understood she could be special. But while she shared traits with Andre Agassi or Jim Courier or Marcelo Rios or the Williams sisters, Nick could explain all the things that made her different. The biggest difference? Unlike players who needed to be pushed through practice, young Maria was incredibly regimented and could lead her own practices. So Nick had to accept that even though he was the most respected coach in the game, there would be days when he didn't talk much.

Every coach I've worked with has their own style, but the best ones share a lot of the same characteristics. They're adaptable. They aren't afraid to challenge widely held assumptions. They aren't focused as much on winning as they are drawing the best performance out of their players—which, in turn, leads to wins.

What is a manager in the business world if not a coach? This person has multiple people working under them, and their responsibility is to extract a great performance from those employees every day. The best bosses, you'll notice, also seem to share some of the same traits I listed for some of the best coaches. The worst bosses, meanwhile, share the same traits as some of the least successful coaches. They're stubborn. They believe they're always the smartest person in the room. They insist on doing everything the way it has always been done.

That last one is an absolute killer from a coach or from a boss (or from a parent). A willingness to evolve is what allows an organization to keep winning. It's funny that Alabama football coach Nick Saban has a reputation as an old-school hard-ass. Don't get me wrong. He can definitely be a hard-ass. But you won't meet many coaches more willing to adapt to changing times. I learned that when he hired me while he was coaching the Miami Dolphins in 2005. A coach who always wanted to do the same old thing the same old way never would have hired a snot-nosed, twenty-something mental conditioning consultant. But Nick thought training his players' brains could help them perform better.

Later, at Alabama, he completely changed his offensive and defensive philosophies to keep up with changes in the game. The 2011 team that won the national title tried to squeeze the life out of teams with its defense. The offense's job was to score enough and eat enough clock to not screw it up for the defense. Nick's 2020 national championship team lit up the scoreboard with an aerial assault of an offense that looked like the kind of schemes that would have made Nick throw up ten years earlier. The defense was still good, but its job wasn't to dominate anymore. Opposing offenses had evolved to the point that no defense could be as dominant as Alabama's was in 2011. Alabama's 2020 defense needed to force the occasional turnover, kill a few opposing drives with sacks, and generally not screw it up for the offense. A few of Nick's former assistants—not Kirby Smart or Mel Tucker, thankfully—did not take this lesson with them when they became head coaches. Some of those former assistants tried to re-create Nick's program from a bygone era (usually whenever it was they worked with him) rather than understanding that adaptability is the most important piece of the puzzle.

Maria Shriver has learned to adapt in her many supervisory roles. She explained that she used to be more of a taskmaster. She believes that stemmed from her early career in broadcast journalism when she was one of very few women in the industry. "All of the women who were entering the workforce had to be as smart as men, as tough as men, work harder than men, dress like men, act like men," she said. "If you took a day off, you felt like the weight of every woman who was going to come behind you on your shoulders." When Maria got pregnant in 1989 with Katherine, the oldest of her four children, Maria asked about maternity leave. She was told there was no maternity leave. "That doesn't happen," she said. "Someone will come along and take your job."

So Maria adopted the mindset of the industry around her. But as she has grown as a leader and worked in different industries, she has learned that there are other ways to help people succeed. Now she starts meetings by checking in with her employees to see where they are emotionally. Her goal now is to "more gently push them forward. I've become more emotionally intelligent," she said.

That last phrase is absolutely critical. If you're leading people now, you might have to lead Baby Boomers, Gen X-ers, millennials, and Gen Z-ers at the same time. These are very different groups that require very different coaching styles. Working with college football teams, I've witnessed a lot of frustration as Boomer and Gen X coaches try to reach millennial players. The least successful coaches are the ones who simply write off that entire generation as soft. The most successful coaches are the ones who can meet those players where they are. Nick Saban, Kirby Smart, and Mel Tucker don't take it easy on their players, but they do recognize that a teaching style that connects with players born in the early 2000s is different than the teaching style that connected with Nick, who was born in 1951, or with Kirby or Mel, who were born in the 1970s.

Aaron Feld is the strength coach for the Oregon football program. If you've ever watched the Ducks play, you've seen him on the sideline. He's the giant dude with the handlebar mustache. He looks like the guy who would be holding up a barbell with one hand on the label of a bottle of questionable tonic in the late nineteenth century. Aaron is more than happy to let people think that he's some macho lunkhead because he looks like he can bench press a Volkswagen. But the truth is, he's always looking for an edge when it comes to reaching his players. He started out the kind of coach who aggressively challenged everyone in the weight room. But as he worked his way up the ranks as an assistant at Alabama-Birmingham and at Georgia, Aaron realized he needed to tailor his approach to each player's individual motivational style. Some players need to be pushed and challenged constantly. They have that Marty McFly "Don't call me chicken" mentality. Some need to be told exactly why they're being asked to do each lift or drill. Once they understand how it can help them on the field, their resistance fades. Some are already so internally motivated that they need to be pulled back at times to keep from burning themselves out. And all of them, Aaron realized, train harder when training is fun. So he created events like Flex Friday and the forty-five-day Fill the Sleeves Challenge, which asked players and staff members to do some kind of biceps and triceps work every day for forty-five days to force those shirt sleeves to get tighter. These concepts also kept players smiling and engaged even while they pushed their bodies to the limit.

That kind of evolution is critical, and that's why it hasn't been limited to sports. It has happened in the military as well.

I met Captain Tom Chaby in 2009 when I was working at
IMG Academy, and Tom was training SEALs at the Naval
Amphibious Base Coronado near San Diego. I had met some
incredible performers in my life, but their wins came in very
controlled environments. Captain Chaby was on another level.
As a SEAL, he had led teams on missions in sixty different
countries. He'd run counter drug operations in South America.
Not long after the September 11th attacks, he deployed to
Afghanistan with a task unit of fifty SEALs. They were among
the first American troops on the ground. In Fallujah, Tom led
a task force of more than four hundred people. He was the
deputy commanding officer of SEAL Training Command when
we met. Needless to say, I was a little intimidated when he and
Commander Tom Schibler came to meet me to see whether
there was anything my work could offer one of the world's
most elite military units.

Chaby, who has since retired from the navy and began training
business leaders and athletes, has always been a big believer in
process over outcome. That's the bedrock of what I teach, and
it makes sense that he would prefer it. When you have to go
into so many life-and-death situations, how can you not favor
process over outcome? Some of the potential outcomes are too
scary to even consider. Chaby thought my work with athletes
would give me instant credibility with the operators he trained.
A SEAL walking into a room full of football players has the
attention of the room instantly. He figured that someone Nick
Saban would hire to work with his team would have the instant
attention of all the football fans who also happened to be elite,
badass soldiers.

Chaby and Schibler wound up bringing me and several other people from the athlete development world to Coronado to meet with the leaders of the SEAL community. They wanted to know what we taught athletes that could help SEALs perform better. Besides being one of the great honors of my life, this was part of a broader approach by the branches of the armed forces to treat their special operations troops more like athletes. The sports world had been ahead of the military in recognizing the value of training elite performers from a physical, mental, and medical standpoint, and the leaders in the special operations community were intent on catching up. They had created programs to help injured operators rehab like athletes, and those operators occasionally rehabbed alongside elite athletes. They had revamped their training. It still looked more like a far more advanced and difficult version of boot camp than it did an NFL training camp, but it was evolving as the leaders recognized they could achieve their goals—and probably get better operators—with a slightly different approach.

One of the surprising things Tom explained about getting into the SEALs is that it's less about swimming than it is about running. When Tom went through SEAL training in 1990, those who got shin splints got themselves bounced out of the program. They were labeled as weak. Now, the first piece of the Basic Underwater Demolition/SEAL Training program that hopefuls go through at the Naval Special Warfare Preparatory School in Great Lakes, Illinois, helps teach candidates how to avoid shin splints before they ever get to Coronado. The candidates also are taught weight training and swim techniques that will help them perform better when they face the real tests in California. Back in Tom's day, they didn't give away any secrets. Today, the navy wants the best candidates to become SEALs, and leaders don't want them washing out of training for an avoidable reason.

Navy leaders also want those SEALs trained in a way that helps identify the best candidates. "We started realizing that waking a class up at 2 a.m. with a bunch of instructors just lighting you up served very little purpose other than hazing," Tom said. "Instead, we just increased the standards and then gave them the strategies to navigate those standards. If they met the standards, that's all we wanted. We weren't going to reduce the standards. That's unacceptable. But we gave them the tools to meet the standards."

So while the instructors may not be barging into the barracks to wake up the candidates (unless it's Hell Week), the training is probably more difficult. Tom isn't sure he'd be selected for the program now. He was a football player and competitive skier growing up, so he had a pretty impressive resume. But now, he said, the navy is looking for elite athletes. You'd better have won a conference title in something in college.

This philosophical shift isn't that different from the best football coaches of this era ditching three-a-day practices and dog-cussing players. Some people romanticize those brutal practices, but the fact is that a good Alabama player now would destroy a good Alabama player in the same position from 1965. Bear Bryant's practices in August may have been harder than Nick Saban's, but Nick Saban's practices are still hard.

And Saban's player is getting the best nutrition and the best medical care and has a GPS device embedded in his shoulder pads to measure his workload at practice. Saban's player also is completing weight-room workouts in the off-season that would make the average person cry. Bryant's guy wasn't doing that. So let's say our two hypothetical players are offensive linemen. The player today is at least fifty pounds heavier. He's significantly stronger. He's also probably still quicker and faster than the undeniably tough guy from the Bryant era. The guy from the '60s would look at the guy from today and wonder if we'd started building humans in labs. And he wouldn't have a chance at competing with the guy from today on the football field.

The idea isn't to create softer football players or softer SEALs. It's to optimize the capabilities of both so they can perform their best when it matters most. And when it matters most for a SEAL, it matters a lot more than it matters for any athlete. So while a football coaching staff may tell the offense to pretend it's down five points facing fourth-and-12 with 57 seconds remaining, SEAL instructors design far more elaborate scenarios to simulate the situations their candidates might find themselves in if they finish the program. "Our job," Tom explained, "is to manufacture adversity and pressure and create situations where they have incomplete information, lack of resources, and lack of time, and they have to produce results."

Tom wanted to help candidates learn some of the same process-over-outcome mental techniques that Saban teaches his players. Only instead of not worrying about beating Auburn but focusing on all the steps required to perform their best against

Auburn, Tom wanted candidates to stop worrying about getting through Hell Week and start worrying about performing their best in their next evolution.

What's an *evolution*? In SEAL training, it's one activity out of many in a given day. The first three evolutions of a day might be a five-mile run to breakfast, eating breakfast, and paddling a boat around Coronado. Tom points out that in the SEAL world, breakfast counts as an evolution because instructors may manufacture some adversity there. In the field, SEALs can't just run to First Watch for an omelet. The candidate who tries to look ahead to the end of Hell Week may wind up ringing the bell and leaving the program. The candidate who can stay neutral and focus only on the five-mile run, then breakfast, then the boat expedition, then whatever else comes next has a chance.

That candidate has to meet an even higher standard than the elite operators who came before. But that candidate also gets more evolved coaching than the operators who came before. And that makes one of the strongest organizations even stronger.

Maria Shriver was so right. You can make your organization— whether it's your business or your family—stronger by leading it like a coach. And you'll be able to coach your coworkers and your children better if you're living neutrally. Remember, neutral thinking is all about going to the facts and removing your feelings. In supervisor-subordinate and parent-child relationships, emotions can get pretty heated. The more information you arm yourself with, the better you can take those emotions out of these encounters, go to the truth, and find a next right step that helps everyone.

The first step is to identify the person's strengths and weaknesses. This is critical in any walk of life, but it might seem a little harsh to be creating a draft report on the members of your team in the office. It doesn't need to be that formal, but you do need to measure the people who work under you relative to what the expectations of their jobs are. This doesn't mean you're going to fire the underperformers. You might not even have the power to do that; you certainly don't if we're talking about you managing your kids as a parent. Your goal is to create an honest evaluation so you can create a plan to make the person even stronger where they're already strong and shore up any weaknesses they may have. The difference between when you do it at your job and when my friend Lawrence Frank does it at his job as president of the Los Angeles Clippers is that you won't have Stephen A. Smith and Kendrick Perkins breaking down all your decisions live on ESPN.

This type of blunt evaluation is accepted in the sports world because the process is codified in every sport. In some ways, player evaluation and acquisition has become a spectator sport in its own right. In football and basketball, high school players are broken down by college coaches as those coaches decide whether to spend a valuable resource (one of eighty-five scholarships they're allowed to give as a football coach or one of thirteen as a basketball coach) on that player. This process is followed by a not insignificant number of fans, many of whom pay $10 a month to recruiting network websites to keep track of how well or how poorly the coach is stocking their favorite team.

Meanwhile, the NFL draft industrial complex has grown massive. The draft itself is now televised on ABC, ESPN, and the NFL Network, and media companies get three solid months of content as they examine, often in minute detail, why a quarterback would fit with the Dolphins but not the Broncos, or why an edge rusher from Arizona State should be selected ahead of an edge rusher from Kentucky. In the NBA, it's free agency—the acquisition of players who are already in the league—that gets far more attention than the draft. In the off-season in 2019, Lawrence pulled off one of the biggest coups in free agency. The Clippers signed Kawhi Leonard just after Leonard had led the Raptors to an NBA title. In the same off-season, the Clippers signed Paul George, who had been the best player on the Oklahoma City Thunder. This required massive amounts of player evaluation from Lawrence and his team as they decided which current players would fit with Leonard and George and which ones they needed to trade or let walk in free agency. They also had to determine which complementary pieces to add either through free agency or through the draft.

For someone like Lawrence, honest, frank evaluation of an employee's worth to the company is considered the most important aspect of his job. For you, that probably isn't the case. But make no mistake, if you lead others, it is a critical part of your job.

Maybe you hate doing annual evaluations because they're a mountain of paperwork. Maybe you hate them because you don't want to hurt anyone's feelings. You need to look at them less as a hassle and more as an opportunity to make everyone stronger. In fact, if you're evaluating the strengths and weaknesses of the members of your team only once a year, you're not doing it nearly often enough.

The New England Patriots have a three-word phrase plastered everywhere throughout their facility: Do Your Job. If you're a leader, part of yours is to make sure everyone else does theirs well. And that requires constant evaluation.

Let's say you work in accounting and you have an associate who makes sloppy mistakes that you then must spend time hunting down and correcting. Everything else about this person is fine. They're pleasant. They get along with everyone in the office. They get their work in on time. They don't cause any other problems. Should you wait until the annual evaluation to point out the sloppy mistakes? Or should you figure out why they're happening and work to stop them?

Of course the answer is to address the issue in real time. Imagine Michigan State coach Mel Tucker has a defensive end who does most aspects of the job well but loses containment and lets the quarterback around the edge with the ball a few plays a game. Mel isn't going to bench that player forever. He may not be able to bench him at all because he might not have a better option at the moment. Mel and his defensive line coach are going to examine all those plays when the player didn't keep containment and try to figure out why. Maybe he is guessing on read option plays about whether the quarterback or tailback will wind up with the ball. That isn't what he's taught to do, but he's doing it. So what's the solution? Teach him again until it sticks. Practice defending read-option plays. Every time he guesses the tailback is getting the ball and loses containment because he went chasing that player, stop the play and correct him. When he doesn't guess and stays where he needs to be, praise him. Keep doing this until you're sure that the next time he faces that situation in a game, he keeps containment. He'll know it's working because he won't be watching a QB gallop past him for a first down.

In the office situation we described, the first step is that the associate needs to know they're making mistakes. This may sound overly simplistic if you're already an effective leader, but a lot of supervisors will fix the mistakes without telling the subordinate they're making errors. This, of course, won't fix anything. The conversation may not be entirely pleasant, but if you approach it with the idea that you're trying to help the associate rather than reprimand the associate, that should make it easier. Once you've established that mistakes are being made, you need to dig deeper to find out why they're being made. Is something distracting the associate? Is something going on at home that is weighing heavily on the associate's mind? Or maybe it's something as simple as the coworkers immediately surrounding the associate can get pretty rowdy and make it difficult to concentrate. If this is the case, first you tell the nearby coworkers to cool it. You also can suggest the employee toss some Mozart on their phone and plug in their headphones. Offer to let the person move to a more secluded spot if one is available. Or maybe your company doesn't require everyone to work at the office anymore. If it doesn't affect productivity, maybe you let that person work from home a few days a week.

Good coaches and good bosses have to be their own brand of forensic accountants. They have to find the root cause of the problem and then make corrections throughout the system to ensure they're generating the correct answers. This is easier when the problem is traceable to an error or a misunderstanding of a concept. It's not so easy when the problem is behavioral.

Coaches spend most of their time on a relatively small percentage of players. Most players want to work hard and want to perform as instructed so they can play better. But a few players—and often some of the most talented ones—require the lion's share of the coach's attention. Perhaps the player is so good that they resent their teammates for not being as talented. Perhaps the player doesn't feel they should be required to train as hard since they can already outperform opponents. Or maybe the player is just in a bad mental place and doesn't want to listen.

The behavioral issues also will be the most challenging ones you face as a manager and especially as a parent. In the latter case, you're probably going to have a kid who tunes you out at some point. You may have an employee that does the same. The key in either case is to try to understand the person well enough to find a way to reach them.

It can be incredibly frustrating when someone won't follow the simplest instructions. You just want to yell until they finally say, "Okay, I'll do it." But that won't usually work. The best coaches will tell you that the most difficult part of their jobs is tailoring their messages so that they reach everyone.

Doing that requires knowing how the person you're dealing with is motivated. Are they a pleaser? Then expressing your disappointment might be enough to get through to them. But if they're one of the people I described above—a talented person who knows they have something special—they're probably going to make you work harder. If you've been doing your job as a coach/leader, you've been talking to this person and learning about their history, home life, and aspirations. That should give you some idea of what motivates them.

Is it money? Then explain how working within the flow of the team will allow their talent to shine through, which could lead to promotions or other companies bidding for their services. Is it recognition? Then start publicly applauding this person when they follow instructions and do their job well. Withhold that public applause when they don't, and explain why you're withholding it.

Do they just need to be told why? This is a really common one with athletes, employees, and angry teenagers. You're probably going to face this one more as a parent, but there is a point at home and at the office when "because I said so" is not only the wrong answer but is just going to piss off the other person even

more. In chapter 1, I told you about pro tennis player Taylor
Dent, who cross-examined his coaches about every single thing
they asked him to do. He wasn't doing that to be a pain in the
ass even if he seemed like a pain in the ass when he was doing
it. He did it because he wanted to understand why. His whole
life was invested in his tennis career, so he felt like the least
his coaches could do was explain why they have him doing
drill X instead of drill Y. You can defuse a lot of tense situations
at work and at home by providing more information so that
everyone understands why certain decisions get made and why
certain instructions are given.

No matter the situation, no matter who the other person is, you
can help both of you by leading the way a good coach would
lead. Go to the facts. Find the issue. Find the next right step.
Show that person you want to help them get better.

Everyone can use a great coach. But that isn't limited to the
people who work for you. You need a great coach too. And who
is the best coach for you? The person who knows you better
than anyone—yourself.

Just as we can't fire our kids, we can't fire ourselves. So
we've got to figure out how to coach ourselves. To truly live
neutrally, you need to understand your own influence on
yourself. You need to be able to equip yourself with the truth.
That means you must stop making negative statements—both
in your head and out of your mouth. That means you need
to go to the facts instead of letting your feelings guide your
decisions.

Would you want to use unhinged emotion to make an important decision for your team at work or for your children? Of course you wouldn't. So use some of the same tactics we discussed earlier in this chapter on yourself. Recognize how you're motivated and motivate yourself that way. When you screw up, don't just scream at yourself. (Especially not in public.) Talk to yourself the way you would a coworker who made a mistake. Examine the facts and figure out a way to get better.

That's what great coaches do—with their teams and with themselves.

# CHAPTER 11

# THERE IS NO FINISH LINE

Billy Donovan had just reached the pinnacle of his chosen profession, and it didn't feel like he thought it would. His Florida basketball team had been unranked to start the 2005–2006 season, but the Gators morphed from pleasant surprise to dominant favorite to national champs. For a guy who started coaching college basketball at twenty-four and got his first head-coaching job at twenty-eight, going to Indianapolis for the Final Four and cutting down the nets above a confetti-strewn floor was *the* dream, and Billy had just achieved it at age forty.

It felt as if his whole life had been directed toward that one goal, so he was surprised when he didn't feel completely fulfilled. Hadn't he just achieved the thing he'd spent most of his life chasing? It dawned quickly on Billy that he needed to look at his world differently. "If you think you're going to be whole as a person, you're not," he said. "It's not the end-all, be-all."

You probably have goals for your life. Maybe your list looks something like this:

- Outsell everyone else at the company

- Become the boss

- Make a million dollars

But what happens if you accomplish all three? Does a banner drop down from the ceiling? Can you just go home and sip drinks by the pool every day for the rest of your life?

Conversely, you might have goals to overcome challenges in your life. Maybe your list looks like this:

- Get through this divorce

- Find a better job

- Beat the C-word

Accomplishing those goals would be massive victories. But just like the goals listed above them, they're outcomes that don't necessarily determine what comes next. Once you reach them, what then?

We can't focus all our energy on a few far-off outcomes or we risk feeling empty when we finally get there. Or worse, we're completely devastated when we fail to reach them.

If you're living neutrally, you won't fall into this trap. You'll celebrate the victories when they come and then move on to the next moment. You'll curse the defeats when they come and then move on to the next moment. My dad defined us not as human beings but as human becomings. We're not meant to be stagnant. We constantly evolve, even after we think we've reached the pinnacle of our existence.

Billy grasped that very quickly after that first national title. He didn't allow himself to feel unfulfilled for long. He went back to work, and he made sure everyone in his orbit also understood that they hadn't crossed any sort of finish line in Indianapolis. There was more to do. And that next year helped Billy evolve.

Florida stars Joakim Noah, Al Horford, and Corey Brewer—who probably would have been lottery picks in the 2006 NBA draft—had decided to come back for another season to chase a second national title. So Billy sought the advice of people who had achieved tremendous success. He didn't want to know how they won. He wanted to know what happened *after* they won. He visited with Pat Riley, who had coached the Lakers to NBA titles in 1982, 1985, 1987, and 1988 and who had just coached the Miami Heat to a title in 2006. He visited with Bill Belichick, who had coached the Patriots to Super Bowl wins in 2001, 2003, and 2004 (and who would win a few more). Closer to home, he quizzed Florida soccer coach Becky Burleigh, who led her team to a national title as a young coach in 1998.

Billy wanted to know how to handle success. Everyone came at it from their own perspective, but the advice from all these accomplished coaches was to treat the new season like an entirely new experience. The chase for a second national title couldn't be a continuation of the first one. It would have its own life.

In the first meeting for the 2006–2007 team, Billy brought in a guest speaker. Sociologist Harry Edwards had talked to the team before and made an impact, and Billy hoped Edwards's message would resonate this time. Edwards drew a mountain on a white board with a basketball at the top. He said the Gators probably thought they were at the top of that mountain because they'd just won the national title and brought back mostly the same team. Then he hit them with the truth. They weren't at the top of the mountain. They weren't even at the base of the mountain. They'd need to walk a long way to even get to the mountain.

Basically, they were back where they were the previous year when no one expected them to win a national title. But Edwards pointed out that they'd have to take a different route up the mountain this time. No one expected anything from them a year earlier. Now everyone expected another national title. That meant there would be more obstacles in the path, including opponents hoping to topple a No. 1-ranked team, or complacency after already winning a title. This journey would require more careful navigation.

Billy thought the players received the message well, but, that summer, he realized how different his journey might be. Noah, Horford, and Brewer—three coachable, team-first players who had become stars in part by never acting like stars—suddenly had some issues they needed to discuss. Donovan had scheduled two exhibition games in Canada that September, which under NCAA rules would allow the Gators to get in several days of early practices in Gainesville before the official start to the preseason in October.

The trio came to Billy's office and asked if the Gators could skip the Canadian tour. Billy didn't get mad. He just asked why. Horford explained that this veteran team probably didn't need an extra ten days of two-and-a-half-hour practices. (Al might have been a little conservative. Billy could run some long practices back then.) Billy thought back to a conversation with Florida volleyball coach Mary Wise, whose team had reached the national title game in 2003 but then lost in the second round of the NCAA Tournament in 2004. Mary had told Billy she'd tried too hard to control everything in that next season, and it wound up hurting the team. So Billy decided that this season's journey would require him to cede some control.

Okay, he told the players. What if each practice is only an hour? Fifteen minutes of offense. Fifteen minutes of defense. Fifteen minutes of press. And fifteen minutes of special situations. The players seemed amenable. But there was a catch, Billy said. It would be up to those three to make sure everyone practiced at a championship level. If they didn't, each practice would start over at the end of the first hour. The players relished that responsibility, and no practice ahead of the Canadian tour lasted longer than an hour.

Late in that season, Billy faced another crossroads. After a win against South Carolina, his players complained that they just weren't having any fun. The previous season had been a blast. The current season—carrying the weight of national title expectations—had been a slog. So Billy said that from that point forward, they would party in the locker room after every win as if they'd just won the national title. It didn't matter if they beat a good opponent by thirty or a bad opponent by one, they would savor the moment. The Gators didn't get a chance to celebrate right away. They lost their next two games. But then they ripped off ten wins in a row, beating Kentucky, sweeping through the Southeastern Conference Tournament, and then rolling through the NCAA Tournament, where they ultimately beat Ohio State in Atlanta to win that second national title.

Billy knew after going into that second title run that fulfillment wouldn't come from the championship itself. It would come from the journey. "A trophy or a ring, to me, is just a sign of a bunch of people pulling together to accomplish something extraordinary," Billy said. "If you think that any of those things is going to fulfill your life, it's not. Those accomplishments are great, but the next day, life is going on."

Life went on for Billy. He thought after that season he wanted to try his hand at the NBA and coach the Orlando Magic, but he changed his mind two days later and wound up coaching at Florida for eight more years. In 2015, he finally was ready to make the jump to the NBA with the Oklahoma City Thunder. And he entered it with a different perspective. He savored his chance to work with Kevin Durant and Russell Westbrook and Chris Paul. In 2020, Billy took over the Chicago Bulls. I think he's going to win an NBA title eventually. When he does, he'll know it's not the be-all and end-all. It'll be another step in an incredible journey.

Taking that next step remains the most important part of living neutrally. We can't let anything—not success, not failure, not fear—keep us from it.

When I was in my twenties, I drove from Los Angeles to Florida to start a new life. Everything went smoothly through Arizona and New Mexico and most of Texas. Then, just outside Beaumont near the Louisiana border, a tire blew on my U-Haul trailer. The blowout sent me spinning across the road for a few terrifying seconds. I wound up safe on the shoulder, and fortunately all that out-of-control metal hadn't hit anyone else.

My dad hooked me up with a friend of his from the self-esteem movement named Bernell Lovett. Bernell, the mother of country singer and one-time Julia Roberts spouse Lyle Lovett, lived in suburban Houston. She took me in while I got the tire fixed. Once it was fixed, I gripped the wheel tight and got back on the road. I didn't want to be in that driver's seat anymore. I had covered half of America without seeing a single skid mark on the road. Now all I could see were the skid marks. How many of them had led to fiery crashes? How many had led to deaths?

Long before I put a name to neutral thinking, I had to find a way to get back there. I couldn't think about how far I still needed to drive or I'd never make it, but I still needed to keep going. I had a new teaching job in Florida, and I couldn't let the fear the blown tire created keep me from my future. So I kept driving, one mile at a time, one county at a time, one state at a time. The asphalt kept buzzing under my wheels, and eventually I made it to Florida.

That word *asphalt* reminds me of a video I came across of my dad. You can still find it on YouTube today.[1] He was talking to a crowd about how to feel incredible, which seems astounding to me because I know he was years into his fight with the C-word when he spoke to this group.

"Would you like to be incredible every day?" my dad asked the crowd. "Then do what I do. Maintain a low standard. Any day on this side of the asphalt is all it takes for me to have a terrific day. We have friends on the other side of the asphalt that would love to have a shot at a bad day."

This was my dad. He preached positive until the end. But even though we never got a chance to talk about it, I think he would have loved the idea of living neutrally. Because at his core, that's how he lived. "I'm 100 percent responsible for my large, moderate, small wins as well as losses," he told that crowd. "And a lot of people don't like to hear that. They don't want to be put in charge."

We're all in charge of our wins and losses because we're in charge of what we do next. And we have to understand that there's always a next. There is no goal you can achieve that allows you to simply power down. There is no failure so awful that you can melt into a bush never to be seen again. So as you look into your future, don't assign so much weight to things that haven't happened yet. Never say, "If I could just do this, everything will be wonderful." Never say, "If that happens, I'm done." Neither one is true.

A few days before my first major surgery in 2020, I sat in a church parking lot. I turned the phone on myself because I wanted to log how I was thinking in that moment. "One of the interesting parts of this neutral approach sometimes is you're almost afraid to be optimistic," I said. "As I'm halfway through this process now and I go into the surgery, there's a part of you that wants to start thinking about plans. What you're going to do next. How you're going to feel when this surgery is successful. Then you have this fear of thinking that way, and then it not happening. I realized that's actually negative. I want to be in a situation where I start thinking about this next step—after the divorce, after the book, after the health challenges—just a lot of things that have been hard."

In that video, I downshift to neutral in real time. I'd gone negative, wondering if I should even be making plans. Then I recognized that line of thinking was negative. So I flushed it and started thinking about my next right step. I've done it countless times since.

As of this writing in May 2021, I still haven't looked in a mirror without sunglasses on. Fear is real, even as we do everything within our power to stay neutral and execute the plan in front of us. Life isn't going to get easier. It's always going to be messy. There will always be a C-word or a pandemic or some other unplanned disaster.

I know I'll find the strength soon to take off those glasses and see a different next step. But even as that fear remains, I'm still behaving my way to a better future. I'm following my doctors' instructions. I'm focusing on my health. I'm keeping the faith. I'm trusting the process—one next right step at a time.

And wherever you are on your life's path, I hope that after reading this book you accept all that's happened because you also know that none of what has happened in the past predicts the future. Every moment is its own adventure.

So you own that next moment. And the next. And the next.

And you keep going.

# POSTSCRIPT

## —— BY RUSSELL WILSON ——

You meant the world to me. Ever since we first met, you impacted my life and my world and everyone around it.

The thing that was amazing about you was that you always sacrificed so much for others without even thinking about yourself. You served. You loved. You gave back.

After we didn't win the Super Bowl in February 2015, we flew down to San Diego. We said we were going to start all over. You basically lived with me for a month. I'd wake up at 5 a.m., and you'd be blasting "Oceans" by Hillsong UNITED. That song is about keeping faith no matter how deep the water gets. It was the perfect message for what I was going through, but I realize now you were preparing yourself for what you'd have to go through.

You were able to get closer to God on that journey, and through your toughest times you became the strongest you've ever been.

What I'll miss the most is the confidence and the peace you could bring—in the best moments and also in the hardest moments. This book is a testament to the amazing life of an amazing man.

People always say when someone dies as young as you did that the person left too soon—that they died early. In terms of age, you did. But in terms of people you impacted and changed, you lived an incredibly long life. You were able to multiply everyone else by twenty.

I'm so grateful that you got to know Jesus. I know you're up there shining down with your dad and also with my dad. All three of you are hanging out together, watching me and my career, watching all of us. And I know you're neutral. You're telling me, "Just keep going. Stay the course."

You used to always say the best is ahead. I really believe that. The best is ahead, Trevor.

I love you, Trevor Moawad.

Until we meet again . . .

The Best Is Ahead.

Love,
russell wilson
#3

# ACKNOWLEDGMENTS

HELP OTHERS GET AHEAD. YOU WILL ALWAYS STAND TALLER WITH
SOMEONE ELSE ON YOUR SHOULDERS.

—BOB MOAWAD

A special thank-you to the doctors, nurses, and administrators
of Cedars-Sinai.

Eternal gratitude to Solange Moawad.

A very special thanks to those who have attempted to stay
connected. Words do not come easily. I have struggled to stay
plugged in, and I'm grateful to everyone who tried.

To Andy Staples, Alan Zucker, Shannon Welch, Judith Curr,
and all those at HarperOne and HarperCollins for the chance to
share our ideas.

May the best of the past be the worst of the future.

# NOTES

## CHAPTER 1: WHY NEUTRAL?

1. David Leonhardt, Twitter post, March 12, 2021, 8:45 a.m. https://twitter.com/DLeonhardt/status/1370370254761828359.

2. Victoria Azarenka, interview with Trevor Moawad, *Think About It*, podcast audio, January 26, 2021. https://podcasts.apple.com/us/podcast/trevor-moawad/id1550868229?i=1000506686080.

3. Roy F. Baumeister, Ellen Bratslavsky, Catrin Finkenauer, and Kathleen D. Vohs, "Bad Is Stronger Than Good," *Review of General Psychology* 5, no. 4 (2001): 323–70.

4. Russell Wilson, "My Secret to Staying Focused Under Pressure," filmed May 2021 at Russell Wilson's home, TED video, 6:02. https://www.ted.com/talks/russell_wilson_my_secret_to_staying_focused_under_pressure.

## CHAPTER 4: DETERMINING YOUR VALUES

1.  Russell Wilson, Twitter post, June 1, 2020, 1:04 p.m. https://
    twitter.com/DangeRussWilson/status/1267502287829647360.

## CHAPTER 5: BEHAVING YOUR WAY TO SUCCESS

1.  William McRaven, "Admiral McRaven Addresses the University
    of Texas at Austin Class of 2014," May 23, 2014, YouTube
    video, 19:26. https://www.youtube.com/watch?v=yaQZFhr
    W0fU&t=3s.

2.  Robert Whiting, *The Meaning of Ichiro* (New York: Warner Books,
    2004).

3.  Whiting, *The Meaning of Ichiro*.

4.  Jim Caple, "Ichiro's Bats More Than Pieces of Wood," ESPN.com,
    July 1, 2002. http://a.espncdn.com/mlb/columns/caple_jim
    /1400915.html.

5.  Ichiro Suzuki, "The Art of Preparation," March 29, 2018,
    MLB.com video, 4:53. https://www.youtube.com/watch?v
    =7FXW3xIdwo0.

6.  Allen Stein Jr., "Stephen Curry—Success Is Not an Accident,"
    YouTube video, 3:55. https://www.youtube.com/watch?v
    =rxsdiusm1NQ.

## CHAPTER 6: INDIANA TREVOR AND THE SCROLL OF DOOM

1.  *Indiana Jones and the Temple of Doom*, film directed by Steven
    Spielberg, Paramount Pictures, 1984.

2. "On 'Doomsurfing' and 'Doomscrolling': Can You Think of a Better Way to Spend Your Time?" Merriam-Webster, June 16, 2020. https://www.merriam-webster.com/words-at-play/doomsurfing-doomscrolling-words-were-watching.

3. Molly Cook, Bruce Sacerdote, and Ranjan Sehgal, "Why Is All COVID-19 News Bad News," National Bureau of Economic Research, November 2020. https://www.nber.org/papers/w28110.

4. "Coping with Stress," Centers for Disease Control, January 22, 2021. https://www.cdc.gov/coronavirus/2019-ncov/daily-life-coping/managing-stress-anxiety.html.

5. Vanessa LoBue, "More Than Just Another Face in the Crowd: Superior Detection of Threatening Facial Expressions in Children and Adults," *Developmental Science* 12, no. 2 (2009): 305–13.

6. Vanessa LoBue and Judy S. DeLoache, "Detecting the Snake in the Grass: Attention to Fear-Relevant Stimuli by Adults and Young Children," *Psychological Science* 19, no. 3 (2008): 284–89.

7. Ed Koch, "Reagan's Afterlife on Earth," *Jewish World Review*, June 8, 2004. http://jewishworldreview.com/0604/koch_reagan.php3.

8. Sally C. Curtin, "State Suicide Rates Among Adolescents and Young Adults Aged 10–24: United States, 2000–2018," *National Vital Statistics Reports* 69, no. 11 (2020): 1–9.

9. Kenneth A. Feder, Kira E. Riehm, and Kayla N. Tormohlen, "Associations Between Time Spent Using Social Media and

Internalizing and Externalizing Problems Among US Youth," *Journal of the American Medical Association Psychiatry* 76, no. 12 (2019): 1266–73.

10. Melissa G. Hunt, Courtney Lipson, Rachel Marx, and Jordyn Young, "No More FOMO: Limiting Social Media Decreases Loneliness and Depression," *Journal of Social and Clinical Psychology* 37, no. 10 (2018): 751–68.

## CHAPTER 7: LOCKING ON/LOCKING OUT

1. Rachel Nauen, "Over Half of Employers Lose 1–2 Hours of Productivity a Day," CareerBuilder.com, July 4, 2017. https://resources.careerbuilder.com/news-research/employers-battle-workforce-distraction.

## CHAPTER 9: YOU ARE YOUR OWN GENERAL MANAGER

Ben Cohen, "Alex Caruso: The LeBron of Playing with LeBron," *The Wall Street Journal*, September 18, 2020. https://www.wsj.com/articles/alex-caruso-lebron-james-lakers-nba-playoffs-11600406618.

2. Maria Menounos, interview with Trevor Moawad, *Better Together*, podcast audio, January 27, 2020. https://podcasts.apple.com/us/podcast/40-how-to-gain-control-of-your-life-mind-with-trevor-moawad/id1320060107?i=1000463814867.

## CHAPTER 11: THERE IS NO FINISH LINE

1. T. J. Hoisington, "How Do You RESPOND? with Bob Moawad," July 4, 2020, YouTube video, 6:16. https://www.youtube.com/watch?v=_ySN41P_UMw&t=2s.